ck

Nationalism
and Unionism
in 19th Century
Ireland

R Rees

Colourpoint

For Jack and Isobel

6 5 4 3 2

© Russell Rees and Colourpoint Books
   Newtownards 2001

Designed by Colourpoint Books, Newtownards
Printed by Betaprint

ISBN 1 898392 28 5

Colourpoint Books
Unit D5, Ards Business Centre
Jubilee Road
NEWTOWNARDS
County Down
Northern Ireland
BT23 4YH
Tel: 028 9182 0505
Fax: 028 9182 1900
E-mail: info@colourpoint.co.uk
Web-site: www.colourpoint.co.uk

About the Author

Russell Rees is a graduate of the University of Ulster. He was awarded a PhD for his thesis on relations between Northern Ireland, the Irish Free State and Britain in the period 1945–51. Dr Rees is currently Head of History at Omagh Academy and has written a number of books about Irish history; these include *Ireland and British Politics* (1993), *Union to Partition, Ireland 1800–1921* (1995) and *Ireland 1905–25* (1998), all published by Colourpoint.

Cover Picture:
The funeral of John McConnell passing Hercules Place, Belfast, on 18 August 1864. McConnell was a loyalist who had been mortally wounded by police during a sectarian riot a few days earlier. As his funeral passed Hercules Place, it met with jeers from a nationalist crowd. Although Hussars were present to keep order, shots were fired by loyalists in the funeral procession.

Contents

The Act of Union

HISTORIANS HAVE DEVELOPED the niggling habit of identifying what they regard as a key event or turning point in a country's history and then stressing just how much continuity there was either side of the chosen date. Ireland at the time of the Union certainly conforms to this pattern. Whereas the impact of the Union on Irish social and economic life was minimal, its influence on political developments over the following century was profound. The Union provided the basis for the ideological conflict between unionism and nationalism which was to gather pace as the nineteenth century progressed. It also left Westminster with sole responsibility for the conduct of Irish affairs and, in the decades after the Union, the Irish question was to exert an increasingly powerful influence in British political life. The British government believed that the Union experiment had solved the Irish question and that Ireland would quickly learn to appreciate the benefits, economic and political, which would accrue from the new constitutional relationship. Yet, while the Union created the United Kingdom, it failed to unite the two peoples. The Irish were never committed to integration. Moreover, the rise of Catholic power in the nineteenth century brought the Irish question into sharper focus. Politically, Westminster would have to contend with Catholic grievances, and, economically, the crucial problem of land ownership in Ireland would have to be confronted.

The Act of Union received the royal assent on 1 August 1800 and took effect from 1 January 1801. It abolished the

Irish Parliament which had been located in Dublin's College Green and, thereafter, 100 Irish MPs, 28 Irish peers and four Church of Ireland bishops took their places in the Parliament at Westminster. When Ireland's population at the time is taken into account, such representation can be described as generous. Interim arrangements were made to adjust tariffs between Ireland and Britain, but these had been phased out altogether by 1817. The impact made by these financial changes was negligible, and they merely accelerated the advance of an economic union between the two countries which was already taking shape in the second half of the eighteenth century. Even politically, there was considerable continuity with the pre-Union era. While the removal of the Dublin Parliament provided an obvious break, the whole complex machinery of the Castle administration not only remained in place but substantially increased over the course of the nineteenth century. Clearly, Ireland would not follow the Scottish example and become fully integrated into the United Kingdom system of government.

The chief architect of the Union, William Pitt, the Prime Minister, had indicated that the Union would allow Irish problems to be tackled in a more efficient and sympathetic manner. Ireland would, he argued, enjoy all the benefits which would automatically flow from her new relationship with Britain. Yet, in truth, the Westminster government's decision was not dictated purely by long-term considerations. Although Pitt had been considering a Union for some time, the move in 1800 was primarily an example of crisis management. Ireland had experienced a serious rebellion in 1798 when perhaps as many as 50,000, in places as far apart as County Antrim and County Wexford, fought to free Ireland from British rule. Yet, while all the participants could subscribe to this general aim, it was apparent that they had been motivated by a number of very different factors. The United Irishmen, as their name suggests, saw Presbyterians in the north join forces with

Catholics in the south. This collaboration contributed to the complex mix of urban political radicalism, influenced by recent revolutionary events in America and France, serious agrarian unrest, based on the secret society tradition in rural Ireland, together with a strong conspiratorial element at the heart of the United Irish leadership, all of which combined to produce an insurrection in 1798. Crucially, the conspirators had colluded with revolutionary France and, though a small French invasion force had successfully landed in County Mayo, swift action by the British fleet prevented the main body of French troops from reaching Irish shores.

These events ensured that the long-term better government of Ireland was not the immediate concern when Westminster embarked on its Union project. Fears of a fresh invasion attempt and the need to protect its Irish flank exerted a powerful influence on British thinking. Britain had been at war with France since 1793, and Pitt knew that the French could exploit further unrest in Ireland by launching an invasion, either to divert British attention away from the war on the continent or to provide a bridgehead for a subsequent invasion of the mainland. In these circumstances the Union was the surest way of returning Ireland to stability and reducing the prospect of another invasion attempt. The occasion of the 1798 rebellion provided Pitt with the opportunity to press the case for a Union. In doing so Pitt repeatedly reminded members of the Protestant Ascendancy, the social elite that had dominated Irish society in the eighteenth century, that their survival depended on the security offered by the British state, something which could be more effectively delivered if the two countries were united under a single government. The 1798 rebellion had clearly demonstrated the vulnerability of the Ascendancy class in the face of a popular uprising and its dependence on British forces for protection. Indeed, the British had acted swiftly and decisively in suppressing the rebellion. An elaborate spy network had ensured that the revolutionary movement was kept under tight surveillance, and key leaders were already in custody when the insurrection began. An effective campaign of terror during 1797, led by the army, had already weakened the United Irish organisation in Ulster. Thereafter, a savage military response to the outbreak of revolutionary violence in 1798, followed by systematic and brutal repression, guaranteed a crushing victory for government forces.

In his efforts to persuade the Protestant Ascendancy, whose members dominated the Irish Parliament, to back the idea of a legislative union, Pitt made effective use of the patronage system. New titles were created for a number of Irish MPs, while more were generously compensated in other ways, and this guaranteed a measure of support for the new initiative. However, more Irish MPs were convinced by Pitt's argument that only direct control from Westminster could restore firm government to Ireland and look after the long-term interests of the Ascendancy class. In the wake of the 1798 rebellion, this view was decisive in securing a majority for the Union in the Irish Parliament. Not surprisingly, those members of the Ascendancy who favoured a legislative union were primarily motivated by self-interest. Previously, the Irish Parliament had been successful in defending Protestant interests, but a growing number of the Ascendancy class now believed that this task could be more effectively met by the Parliament in London which was, of course, familiar with the relevant religious arguments. Ironically, a majority of the educated Catholic middle class also favoured a legislative union, believing that it offered the best prospect for the amelioration of Catholic grievances. This had been the message which the British government had been transmitting, as it actively encouraged Catholics to believe that the Act of Union would be followed quickly by legislation which would finally concede Catholic emancipation. Pitt had intended that legislation granting Catholic emancipation would accompany the Act of Union, but he dropped this idea once it became clear that the introduction of such a controversial measure would create major difficulties in both Britain and Ireland. Still, Catholics were hopeful that their claims for just treatment would receive a more sympathetic hearing in the Westminster Parliament, and early progress on this issue was expected.

In addition to the security aspect, Pitt also hoped that the Union would consolidate British control over Ireland and, simultaneously, would improve Anglo-Irish relations by removing the risk of a serious conflict between the Parliaments in London and Dublin. Friction between the two Parliaments was scarcely concealed, and the likelihood of a major constitutional clash had grown significantly in the second half of the eighteenth century. In this period, two particular features influenced the development of Irish politics. Firstly, the Protestant Ascendancy had to confront the growth of Catholic power with the emergence of a small, educated Catholic middle class. Predominantly involved in business and trade, this emerging Catholic middle class had become increasingly important in Irish commercial life, and this contributed to the raising of political consciousness among its members. Not surprisingly, this growing political awareness soon found expression in opposition to the Penal Laws, a series of discriminatory measures directed against the Catholic population. Aimed at consolidating Protestant power following the Williamite victory in the 1690s, the Penal Laws imposed significant social, economic and political constraints on Catholics for most of the eighteenth century. While the impact of the Penal Laws was most keenly felt by the declining Catholic landowning class, the commercial middle class escaped the worst effects of the legislation and encountered few obstructions on their route to economic success. It was this Catholic middle class which led the struggle for the removal of Catholic grievances and, in the last quarter of the eighteenth century, a series of Catholic Relief Acts began the process of dismantling the Penal Laws. By 1793 Catholics, who met the franchise qualification, had won the right to vote and this opened the way to further political progress, even though they were still banned from holding certain public offices.

The second major development shaping Irish politics in this period was the growing hostility between the London and Dublin Parliaments. There had long been suspicion of England's intentions in Ireland among some members of the Ascendancy class, but this was to crystallise into a distinctive 'patriot' faction in the Irish Parliament in the latter part of the eighteenth century. The appearance of this patriot group was predictable. The superior attitude frequently adopted by the English in their dealings with Ireland was bitterly resented by a self-confident social and political elite which assumed that it was, at the very least, the equal of the ruling class in England. In addition, it became increasingly apparent that Irish and English interests were often incompatible. Therefore, the patriot faction's initial political forays focused on the defence of Irish interests and the assertion of Irish rights. These factors contributed to a new awareness of Irishness and a growing spirit of independence among the patriot group and their supporters. The Protestant Ascendancy's brief dalliance with 'patriotism' marks the beginning of political nationalism in Ireland, and though it developed in a different form, as elitist Protestant nationalism gave way to popular Catholic nationalism in the nineteenth century, the central demand for Irish self-government remained constant. Another common strand was the tendency to express one's Irishness in a negative manner, and the anti-English tirades indulged in by the patriot leaders set a pattern which influenced subsequent nationalists.

The clear aim of the patriots was to end Westminster interference in Irish affairs. Although they acknowledged that

Ireland was a possession of the British Crown, the patriots claimed that Ireland was a separate kingdom which should be free to have its own laws made by its own Parliament. By the late 1770s, Henry Grattan, who had only been an MP since 1775, emerged as the leader of the patriot party, and he championed the cause of parliamentary independence, arguing that Ireland was an independent nation under a joint Crown. Of course, this nation was very narrowly defined. While it had a strong cultural and historical dimension, membership of this political nation was confined to that exclusive Protestant caste, or Anglican to be more precise, who were born in Ireland. In advocating legislative independence, these Protestant nationalists were demanding the restoration of Ireland's previous rights which, they claimed, had been gradually whittled down by the actions of the Westminster Parliament. What gave real impetus to the patriot struggle, and created the opportunity for the advancement of the patriot cause, was the conflict between England and her American colonies. Serious differences between the two led to the outbreak of war in 1775, and a series of disastrous military engagements for the British resulted in the loss of the colonies in 1782. The patriot faction in the Irish Parliament was quick to exploit the American conflict. Links between Ireland and America had been forged by large-scale emigration earlier in the century, and Grattan and his followers stressed the parallel between the Irish constitutional situation and the American challenge to British authority, while repeating their assertion that, unlike the colonies, Ireland was demanding nothing new, only the restoration of lost rights. Of course, the success of the American colonists served as a warning to the Westminster government in its dealings with Ireland and made English politicians more willing to listen to Irish grievances. The war with America also had dire economic consequences for Ireland. The Irish economy was already in a depressed state, but the trade restrictions caused by the war greatly exacerbated these difficulties, thereby adding urgency to the political demand for legislative independence.

What tipped the balance in the patriots' favour, however, was the entry of France into the American war in June 1778 on the side of the colonists. Regular troops stationed in Ireland had already been dispatched across the Atlantic, and the French intervention opened up the possibility of an attack on an inadequately defended Irish shoreline. To meet this French invasion threat, the Protestant gentry quickly established Volunteer corps throughout the country. Shortly after their formation the Volunteers numbered close to 40,000, with the rank and file drawn principally from well-to-do Protestants and serving under officers who were generally of landowning stock. Ostensibly, they provided a part-time military force to supplement the depleted regular army and to preserve law and order in the countryside, but they quickly acquired a political significance. By this stage the more militant patriots recognised the potential of an alliance with the Volunteers to press their claims for legislative independence. Although the patriots still constituted a minority in the Irish Parliament, the Volunteers provided them with a national organisation to promote their political aims, while acting as a powerful, and armed, extra-parliamentary force standing behind an increasingly confident patriot leadership. With Grattan and his followers now rallying public opinion throughout the country, the government in London could no longer ignore the situation in Ireland. Under pressure, it moved to relax commercial restrictions on Irish trade, but this only encouraged the patriots to seek further concessions. While a second attempt by Grattan to force legislative independence through the Irish Parliament in February 1782 was unsuccessful, it was apparent that the government could not hold out indefinitely. Both the content of the parliamentary debate and the recent activities of the Volunteers provided an indication of the momentum which the patriot cause had established.

The final piece in the jigsaw arrived with a change of government at Westminster in March 1782. In opposition, the Whigs had encouraged the Irish dissidents. Now in government, they signalled that the patriot demands could expect a sympathetic hearing, and Grattan wasted no time in moving a formal declaration of independence in April 1782. While Ireland was not granted 'legislative independence' in the strictest sense, the patriots had won significant political concessions. The shackles which had inhibited the Irish Parliament's room for manoeuvre were removed, but the change did not produce self-government as the Irish executive remained under Westminster control. In reality, the new constitutional arrangements made little impact on Irish society. The patriots were conservative by instinct, and internal squabbles were soon undermining the unity of purpose so evident in the 'victory' of 1782. Yet 'Grattan's Parliament', as the years 1782–1800 became known, was of major symbolic importance. The concessions won from the British became a source of great pride and the period was marked by a spectacular economic recovery. In addition, the parliament building in College Green became a symbol of national freedom. Moreover, the factors which had brought success to the patriots were not lost on later generations of nationalists. The mobilisation of popular support in Ireland, the fear of a French invasion, Britain's involvement in a major conflict and the collapse of a hostile government at Westminster each combined to advance the patriot cause. Yet the decisive element in Grattan's triumph had been the extra-parliamentary pressure exerted by the paramilitary force of semi-political Volunteers.

The action of the 13 American colonies in declaring their independence from Britain had been a major influence on Ireland. The American war breathed new life into Irish politics and a new political vocabulary emerged. Constitutions, rights, representation, independence and even revolution were now subjects for discussion among the politically conscious. Acutely aware of the constitutional inferiority of the Irish Parliament, the patriots seized the opportunity to end British legislative interference. Although the last two decades of the eighteenth century has been described as a golden age for the Ascendancy class, Grattan's Parliament was not a success. In winning legislative independence and yet maintaining the British connection, Grattan and the patriots had achieved their purpose, but their use of this new freedom was disappointing. They rejected Volunteer demands for parliamentary reform, and they had neither the will nor the foresight to tackle the Catholic question. While the patriots regarded themselves as the Irish nation, this could not conceal the fact that 80 per cent of their fellow countrymen were Catholics whom the Irish Parliament decided should be kept in subordination. While Grattan personally wished to grant full political rights to Catholics, he was clearly in a minority, and the various measures of Catholic relief, notably the act of 1793 which gave the vote to wealthy Catholics, were imposed by Westminster against the determined opposition of the Irish Parliament. In effect, the patriots had won a Protestant Parliament for the Protestant nation, and a very narrowly defined Protestant nation at that. What they offered was a very limited and exclusive form of nationalism, and this was reflected in the Irish Parliament's opposition to reform. In spite of these obvious deficiencies, however, the recovery of Grattan's Parliament became the 'holy grail' for every subsequent constitutional nationalist movement.

The 1798 rebellion and the consequent Act of Union had combined to undermine Protestant nationalism. When challenged by the revolutionary forces of the United Irishmen, the weakness of the Irish Parliament was suddenly exposed. Moreover, the rebellion had highlighted the minority status of the Protestant Ascendancy and raised serious questions about its future security. Against this background, Irish MPs struggled to produce a viable alternative and, therefore, accepted, albeit reluctantly, the British government's case for a Union. In time, it became clear that both the rebellion and the Union had deepened divisions within Ireland. Yet it would have been extremely difficult to predict developments following the implementation of the Union. The rise of popular Catholic nationalism, the decline of Presbyterian radicalism and the movement of all Ascendancy opinion in favour of the Union were each, in their own way, a surprise. While the development of some form of anti-Union sentiment was predictable, no one could be sure what pattern this would follow. Indeed, the picture at the beginning of the nineteenth century was very complex. During the great public debate the Union enjoyed the support of both the Catholic hierarchy and a significant section of the Catholic middle class, but was vociferously opposed by a group of Catholic lawyers. On the other hand, the attitude of the recently formed Orange Order was unclear, with the leadership recommending a neutral stance on the question. And though the great wave of national feeling which swept the country in 1782 had, by this stage, clearly evaporated, many high-profile Ascendancy figures, including Grattan himself, remained opposed to the Union. Therefore, both Protestants and Catholics were divided on their attitude to the Union. What was recognised by those who framed the Union, however, was that if it were to work, there would have to be reconciliation both within Ireland itself and between Ireland and Britain. For this to happen, an early resolution of the Catholic question was essential.

2

The Rise of Constitutional Nationalism

ONE THING THE UNION did not deliver was Catholic emancipation, which would have opened up those remaining public offices still closed to Catholics following the various relief measures. This was in spite of Pitt's firm conviction that the ultimate success of the Union depended on emancipation. His original intention had been to introduce the two measures simultaneously, but he dropped this idea once it became clear that such a two-pronged approach might prevent the passing of the Union. Still, once the Union was in place, Catholics expected emancipation to follow. The Prime Minister duly raised the issue in 1801, but he encountered stiff opposition. The King had always been hostile and Pitt did not enjoy the unanimous backing of his cabinet, but the loudest opposition voice was that of the Protestant Ascendancy in Ireland. While the Union had stripped away some of their power, members of the Ascendancy class clearly retained considerable political influence and they were effective in exerting pressure on the government. In these circumstances Pitt took the easy option and the measure was deferred. This delay was to have a powerful bearing on the development of constitutional nationalism.

After the Union, the Catholic cause was taken up by

Protestant advocates at Westminster. The greatest champion of emancipation in this period was Henry Grattan who had won a Yorkshire seat in 1805, but represented a Dublin constituency from 1806 until his death in 1820. Grattan argued that it was time to end the religious discrimination which belonged to a bygone age, and he claimed to speak with the full backing of Irish Catholics. Support for the measure was increasing steadily at Westminster but, with the opposition lobby still firmly entrenched, the prospect of an early success was not great. In Ireland, meanwhile, Catholics were slow to respond to post-Union developments. They had, of course, expected emancipation to be pushed through Parliament but, even when this did not materialise, their attitude was surprisingly complacent. Indeed, Catholic politics at the beginning of the nineteenth century lacked any semblance of dynamism. For the vast majority of Catholics, the debate on emancipation seemed as distant as the debate on the Union. Neither would, it appeared, have any impact on the lives of the masses. Furthermore, there was disagreement among politically aware Catholics. The surviving Catholic gentry favoured a very restrained and cautious approach to the demand for Catholic rights, hoping that such deference would coax a favourable reaction from the government. The growing professional and business classes, on the other hand, demanded more assertive action. In the years immediately after the Union, this division prevented Irish Catholics from mounting a concerted campaign for the ending of emancipation. By 1810, however, the Catholic middle class was clearly gaining the upper hand, and one of their number, Daniel O'Connell, had emerged as the effective leader of the more radical wing of the Catholic Committee, the body responsible for the promotion of Catholic interests.

O'Connell was born into a Catholic landowning family in County Kerry and educated in France before returning to Ireland to practise as a lawyer. Almost immediately, he was drawn to politics, and in his first public speech in 1800 he famously condemned the Union. Later dubbed the 'Liberator' for his contribution to the winning of Catholic emancipation, O'Connell became the dominant figure in Catholic politics in the first half of the nineteenth century. If Grattan was the first leader of constitutional nationalism in Ireland, it was his successor, O'Connell, who gave it a mass following, though this was to be some time in coming. Grattan and other liberal Protestants continued to press the emancipation case in the House of Commons, but there was frequent disagreement with, and among, Irish Catholics on the exact nature of the concessions which they would have to make in return for emancipation. Specifically, it seemed that the government expected to be given some measure of control over the Catholic Church, particularly in relation to clerical appointments and the payment of the clergy. While this did not present a problem for English Catholics, nor indeed for many of the Irish bishops, O'Connell and his radical followers were adamant that no such concessions would be offered. Although he managed to convince a majority on the Catholic Committee of his argument, O'Connell recognised that both the internal bickering and lack of clear political direction were weakening the push for emancipation. The emancipation campaign, moreover, lacked the drive and energy necessary for success. The Catholic Committee had settled into a rut, operating as an ineffective pressure group dependent on English support, and it failed to deliver success in the first two decades of the nineteenth century.

Dismayed by the lack of progress, O'Connell realised that a new approach was essential if Catholics were to be granted full political rights. His strategy was to mobilise the Catholic masses in support of emancipation. Previously, of course, Catholic agitation had been very narrowly based, something which was partly attributable to the fact that only the Catholic gentry and middle class would benefit directly from an emancipation victory. When O'Connell launched a new Catholic Association in 1823, its leadership consisted of the same elements that had dominated previous emancipation campaigns. Of crucial importance, however, was O'Connell's intention to give the association a wider appeal by ensuring that it would campaign not just solely for emancipation, but would seek to redress Catholic grievances in general. Still, the mobilisation of the masses did not immediately follow the establishment of the new movement. What transformed the situation was the introduction of the 'Catholic rent' in 1824, which allowed new members to become 'associates' of the Catholic Association for the sum of one penny per month. This attracted huge numbers and produced the first mass movement in Irish politics. Money was collected outside church doors on Sundays, under the watchful eye of parish priests, before being forwarded to the movement's Dublin headquarters. Within a year of its launch, £20,000 had been transferred to the Catholic Association's coffers. This dramatic development had two consequences. Firstly, it gave the Catholic clergy an important political role and this cemented the relationship between nationalism and Catholicism. Secondly, it allowed the Catholic masses to experience direct participation in a great national political struggle.

O'Connell's charismatic leadership and burgeoning reputation was another vital ingredient in the spectacular growth of the Catholic political nation. His record was exemplary. O'Connell had opposed the Union from the outset, and he had consistently identified, both politically and in his legal work, with the Catholic cause and the protection of Catholic interests. His great skill was to exploit latent anti-English feeling among the Catholic masses. Previously, rural discontent had been channelled into the myriad of secret societies which continued to play a pivotal role in the Irish countryside. More prominent in periods of economic distress, these secret societies, which often exhibited sectarian undertones, were primarily concerned with specific local issues such as rents, tithes and evictions, but they also provided a forum for, admittedly in a very crude fashion, the expression of political grievances. Moreover, resistance to authority was the common element in all secret societies, and this was reflected among large sections of the population. What was missing was a structure for directing such feeling, and, though O'Connell occasionally condemned the excesses of some secret societies, their existence undoubtedly made some contribution to the establishment of a popular political movement. Another significant factor was the recent expansion of the Catholic Church. Seminaries in Ireland were opened and then reorganised to keep pace with the growing demand for clergy, and many of the new trainees were sons of well-to-do tenant farmers. This tended to produce a priesthood which was more in touch with its flock and was, accordingly, more attuned to political developments taking place in Catholic congregations. Yet this did not mean that the Catholic Church took charge of the popular movement. Leadership was firmly in the hands of O'Connell and his closest colleagues in the Catholic Association, but they recognised the value of collaboration with a sympathetic clergy who could bring with them the organisational benefits of the Catholic Church.

O'Connellism was a new political phenomenon. Although O'Connell can be described as the heir of Grattan, in the sense that he saw no contradiction between promoting Irish nationalism while remaining loyal to the Crown, his movement was much more dependent on popular support. Catholic emancipation became an issue of great symbolic importance, and the engagement of the masses transformed the campaign into a moral crusade. Yet this was never truly national in character, because the bedrock of support for O'Connellism was firmly based in Leinster and Munster. Here there was huge expectation among the peasantry of the benefits for the entire Catholic population which would immediately follow emancipation. In the west, on the other hand, where poverty was endemic, the peasantry were too preoccupied with more mundane matters to have either the time or the will to indulge in politics. The north, moreover, with its strong concentration of Protestants, did not prove fertile ground for the emancipation agitation.

In leading this struggle, O'Connell exploited the profound sense of injustice which had always existed among Catholics but had become more acute since the Union. This injustice had social, economic and political origins, and the perception was that the Union had exacerbated the problems facing Catholics. Moreover, the memory of the savage response of government forces to the 1798 rebellion was lodged in the Irish psyche. Although he firmly rejected the separatist nationalism of the United Irishmen, O'Connell was astute enough to recognise the benefits of sharing a political platform with '98 veterans. Indeed, his speeches at these great public gatherings were frequently uncompromising and were regularly punctuated by violent language in which he heaped abuse both on the British government and on the Ascendancy class in Ireland. Undoubtedly, this contributed to the growth of sectarian feeling which had risen sharply in the first two decades of the nineteenth century. This also enabled O'Connell to castigate the Union itself which, he claimed, had been made on a Protestant basis and was directly responsible for many of the Catholic peasantry's grievances.

A temporary setback for the campaign occurred in 1825 when a group of radical MPs at Westminster proposed a new Catholic Relief Bill, with certain safeguards designed to reassure Protestants. O'Connell's support for the measure drew sharp criticism from his more radical followers in Ireland, and further embarrassment was caused when the bill was defeated in the House of Lords. An angry O'Connell returned to Ireland in the summer of 1825 determined to renew the agitation, but it was at this point that the government moved to crush O'Connellism which, by this stage, was regarded as a dangerous popular movement. The Catholic Association was suppressed, though O'Connell moved quickly to relaunch it as the New Catholic Association, and the campaign intensified. Attempts were also made to prosecute O'Connell for incitement to rebellion, but there was insufficient evidence and the charges were dropped. More aggressive than before, O'Connell now benefited from the assistance of his key followers. Richard Lalor Sheil, another lawyer who would become a prominent MP, had been an early opponent of O'Connell's tactics, but, by 1823, they had joined forces, and Sheil became a powerful and effective advocate of emancipation, playing a prominent role in the mobilisation of the Catholic masses. More importantly, Thomas Wyse, a prominent Catholic merchant, persuaded O'Connell that political progress could be made by utilising those enfranchised Catholics, the 40-shilling freeholders who had been given the vote in 1793, in the 1826 general election. Key constituencies were targeted and, much to O'Connell's surprise, it became clear that Catholic voters could defy instructions from their landlords and vote for the candidate of their choice, usually sympathetic liberal Protestants who backed emancipation. In these years before the secret ballot, the threat of eviction was usually sufficient to pull potentially independently-minded voters into line, but, from 1826, landlords had difficulty in countering concerted action by their tenants. This new development was famously highlighted in the Waterford constituency, where the pro-emancipation candidate, Villiers Stuart, defeated the all-powerful Beresford family's candidate.

The demonstration of Catholic electoral power in 1826 sent shockwaves through both the British government and the Protestant establishment in Ireland. A change of government in 1827 promised an early resolution of the emancipation issue, but the sudden death of the new Prime Minister, George

Canning, and the quick resignation of his equally sympathetic successor, Viscount Goderich, threw everything back into the melting pot. The new government was led by the Duke of Wellington, and both he and the new Home Secretary, Sir Robert Peel, or 'Orange' Peel as he was described by O'Connell, were regarded, somewhat unfairly, as implacable opponents of emancipation. At the same time, O'Connell renewed the emancipation agitation in Ireland and, in the early part of 1828, a series of impressive demonstrations of popular support took place throughout the country. Money was again pouring in from the Catholic rent, and it seemed that O'Connell was set on a collision course with the Westminster government. Matters came to a head that summer when a by-election was held in County Clare. The by-election was called following the appointment of William Vesey-Fitzgerald, one of the MPs for Clare, to the cabinet as President of the Board of Trade. Following the convention of the day, any MP appointed to the cabinet had to resign his parliamentary seat in order to seek re-election. Although Vesey-Fitzgerald was a very popular landowner who had been a supporter of emancipation, the Catholic Association was determined to oppose any parliamentary candidate who supported the Wellington–Peel administration. Only when a suitable candidate could not be found, did O'Connell allow his own name to go forward as Vesey-Fitzgerald's opponent. While the existing oaths of supremacy and abjuration prevented O'Connell taking his seat if elected, there was nothing in the law to stop him contesting the seat, and so the scene was set for a dramatic by-election contest in July 1828.

The Clare by-election was a defining moment in the development of constitutional nationalism. Amid scenes of unparalleled popular excitement, O'Connell's full oratorical powers were unleashed. He lambasted his opponent, tore into the Wellington–Peel government and presented himself as the defender of the Catholic people. In fact, the Clare by-election had strong sectarian undertones, and the Catholic clergy were highly visible in their canvassing for O'Connell. At the end of a dramatic and highly-charged campaign he was declared the victor by 2,057 votes to 982 votes. O'Connell's victory presented the Westminster government with a clear challenge. The prospect of the Clare result being repeated all over Catholic Ireland was one thing, but the possibility of Catholic agitation spilling over into serious violence, if the Conservative government continued to resist emancipation, was another. In reality, therefore, it was this new fear of civil disorder which determined the government's thinking, and a Catholic Emancipation Bill was introduced in February 1829. Despite some last ditch attempts to delay the inevitable, the King reluctantly gave the bill the royal assent on 13 April 1829. O'Connell had won a great victory, though the government attempted to check the power of O'Connellism by raising the franchise qualification from a 40-shilling freehold to a £10 freehold. This dramatically reduced the number of Catholic voters but, in the celebrations which followed, this new restriction was largely ignored. The Catholic political nation was jubilant and, delighted with its victory, the Catholic Association dissolved itself. Not surprisingly, the successful tactics used to prise this concession from the British government would not be forgotten.

The Emancipation Act opened up nearly every public office to Catholics, and a new oath of allegiance replaced the previously unacceptable expressions of loyalty. The main beneficiaries were members of the Catholic middle class. From 1829, some of them could sit in Parliament, while others gradually squeezed into the public positions now open to them. For the peasantry, the foot soldiers of the agitation, however, there was no material gain. It was anticipated that general improvements would follow emancipation, but, in reality, the victory of 1829 only raised Catholic expectations which could not be met, and this was to have an important bearing on the future development of Irish nationalism. Yet the peasantry's participation in the great triumph undoubtedly gave them a new self-respect and, crucially, they became more aware both of their rights and of their numerical strength. In harnessing the masses O'Connell gave expression to these rights, and he recognised that the force of public opinion could be channelled to influence governments, even hostile Conservative ones. Thus, the agitation for emancipation became a great moral crusade, as the government was increasingly challenged by majority opinion in Ireland. Of course, in mobilising the peasantry, O'Connell, true to his liberal principles, was careful to ensure that the movement remained constitutional. Still, there was always the possibility of widespread civil disorder if concessions were not granted, and O'Connell's frequently militant rhetoric only reinforced this potential threat. In the end, this was to prove a decisive factor for the Wellington government, as it weighed up the risk of continued resistance to Catholic demands.

Although O'Connell consistently sought Protestant support during the campaign for emancipation, his oratory frequently aroused sectarian feeling. Much of his success was due to the special bond that he established with the Catholic masses who regarded him as one of their own. It would be wrong, however, to attribute undue blame to O'Connell for the growth of sectarian feeling in nineteenth century Ireland. He led a mass movement which sought to redress a major Catholic grievance, and he relied on local parish priests to undertake much of the organisation at grass roots level. Naturally, this strengthened the relationship between Catholicism and nationalism, but one consequence of this development was the creation of a major obstacle for subsequent leaders of nationalism who wanted to appeal across the sectarian divide. Still, one lesson to be drawn from the emancipation victory was that it had been a triumph for Catholic self-reliance. For nationalists to win concessions, they had to confront the

Westminster government directly, though such a course of action had to be buttressed by powerful agitation in Ireland. In the process, both the government and the Irish Protestant minority were suddenly made aware of the political power of the masses. In particular, the Protestant Ascendancy was alarmed by the unprecedented scale of the agitation, and it became clear that the Union offered their only means of protection from the growing Catholic threat. Yet this should not obscure the fact that O'Connell had involved the masses in constitutional politics and, ultimately, their victory was won in Parliament. Thus O'Connell had laid very firm foundations for constitutional nationalism, and it was this form of moderate nationalism which proved to be the dominant strain in nineteenth century Ireland.

Like Grattan's earlier achievement of legislative independence, Catholic emancipation was of more symbolic importance than practical benefit. The great triumph of 1829 also raised expectations among the new Catholic political nation, which saw it as a crucial first step on the road to an overhaul of the entire economic and political system in Ireland. Clearly, O'Connell had demonstrated that constitutional politics could work: the question now was how would he build on this success?

If the Catholic masses could be mobilised to deliver emancipation, surely they could also be harnessed to win further concessions, perhaps even culminating in the repeal of the Union itself. Here O'Connell had to perform a balancing act. While many of his supporters looked forward to radical social and economic changes, he himself was very conservative in his attitude to structural changes in Irish society. Rather, O'Connell saw improvement based on the attainment of an end to Protestant privilege and what he described as "justice for Ireland", though precisely what this meant he chose not to define. Significantly, in spite of his outstanding qualities, O'Connell knew that his emancipation triumph would only guarantee popular support in the short term and that definite progress on the equality issue was required if he was to retain this support.

O'Connell had always maintained that his great goal in political life was the repeal of the Act of Union. Accordingly, in 1830 he founded the Society for the Repeal of the Union, and it was assumed that a repetition of the emancipation tactics would follow. Yet the two issues were entirely different. Emancipation had enjoyed considerable support in Britain, particularly among Whig MPs, and many liberal Protestants living in Ireland endorsed it. The campaign for repeal, however, aroused fears and suspicions about O'Connell's intentions, and the external support, which the emancipation campaign had enjoyed previously, would be replaced by outright opposition to repeal. Furthermore, the agitation for repeal could neither generate the same support among O'Connell's middle class followers nor spark the same level of interest among the Catholic hierarchy. O'Connell was astute enough to recognise these obstacles and, though money poured in, he did not press the repeal issue hard in this early phase. Indeed, even when the repeal agitation reached a crescendo in the early 1840s, O'Connell consistently refused to spell out precisely what he meant by repeal, a ploy that subsequent Irish nationalist leaders repeated in the Home Rule era. Most likely, repeal would have been based on the restoration of the legislative independence secured by Grattan, but a clear definition was unnecessary and probably would have been counter-productive. Instead, repeal became a rallying cry for O'Connell's nationalist supporters and was presented, as Home Rule would be later in the century, as a cure for all of Ireland's political and economic ills. Equally significant, however, was his measured use of the repeal issue as a lever to squeeze reforms out of a frequently unenthusiastic Westminster government. Therefore, O'Connell was prepared to alter his approach depending on the prevailing circumstances in Britain and Ireland.

When prospects looked brighter, as they did in November 1830 when the Whigs returned to power, O'Connell would don his parliamentary hat and press the case for reform at Westminster. Although he never lost his fundamental belief in repeal, O'Connell was pragmatic enough to appreciate the value of achievable, incremental gains which he could present to his followers as progress in his quest to bring justice to Ireland. Only when this reform avenue was firmly closed, did O'Connell virtually abandon Westminster and commit himself exclusively and unequivocally to repeal agitation. During the 1830s, however, a decade of Whig domination, O'Connell concentrated on parliamentary activity, as he pushed for reform. Another factor influencing his decision to adopt a gradualist approach was the level of strife over large parts of rural Ireland in the early 1830s. To some extent he was responsible for this new wave of agrarian unrest, as his successful emancipation campaign had encouraged the belief that the redress of particular economic grievances was imminent. Furthermore, O'Connell had inadvertently demonstrated that direct action could resolve particular problems. In this instance rural discontent focused on the tithe, a tax paid by certain tenant farmers to support the established church, the Church of Ireland. The fact that most of those who were paying for the upkeep of the Church of Ireland were not members of this alien church only added to the sense of injustice felt by Catholics. Anti-tithe protests had been a feature of Irish rural society for some decades, but the level of disturbance generated by the agitation in 1831–33 led to government fears that the situation would quickly degenerate into chaos unless resolute action was taken. Tension was never far from the surface in rural Ireland, and any downturn in agriculture could provoke turmoil.

The anti-tithe protest began in Leinster, though quickly spread to other parts of the country, and it sparked off violent clashes between the peasantry and the authorities. Agrarian secret societies expanded rapidly, and violence reached a peak in 1832 when 242 murders were committed. The government responded with a series of coercive measures, and troops were used to assist the over-stretched police force in maintaining order. The government's tough security measures were backed up by a number of reforms which brought improvements in areas such as education, and also attempted to tackle the tithe issue.

The effect of this carrot and stick policy, a formula repeated by later Westminster governments when confronted by serious agrarian unrest, was to prevent a dangerous situation spiralling out of control. For O'Connell, who was very concerned at the level of social disorder, the Whig government's apparent willingness to consider reform offered the possibility of progress. He was anxious that repeal agitation would not be confused with the anti-tithe protests, because, while there were political advantages to be gained from identifying with a popular cause, the threat to his political leadership from the activities of secret societies engaged in widespread intimidation and violence was obvious. As expected, O'Connell condemned government repression, but he was hopeful that Ireland's inclusion in the government's great scheme of parliamentary reform would allow him to increase his influence at Westminster. O'Connell was bitterly disappointed with the content of the 1832 Irish Reform Act. It gave Ireland only five additional seats, taking the total to 105, and it failed to return the franchise to 40-shilling freeholders who had lost the vote in 1829. Denouncing Earl Grey's administration, O'Connell made repeal the dominant issue in the 1832 general election and, despite the restricted franchise, 39 MPs pledged to support repeal were returned from Irish constituencies.

O'Connell now stood at the head of a party of 39 'Repealers', which included a generous sprinkling of his own family members, but it was soon apparent that the new House of Commons was no more sympathetic to the idea of repeal than the unreformed pre-1832 version. In addition, though repeal may have enjoyed great popular support in Ireland, most Irish MPs were absolutely opposed to any tampering with the Union. In these circumstances O'Connell opted for a policy of keeping repeal agitation ticking over in Ireland, while cooperating with Grey's new Whig administration in an attempt to secure specific reforms. This appeared the most effective way to use his political influence in London. The O'Connellite party was never the powerful instrument that Parnell had at his disposal in the 1880s, but this block of supporters gave him the opportunity to make a decisive intervention if the right parliamentary circumstances existed, and they did lay the foundations for the development of an independent Irish party at Westminster. In spite of the difficulties he encountered with Grey, O'Connell's overall strategy of using repeal to squeeze reform out of a reluctant government appeared to have some success. In 1833 the government at last recognised the need to look at the position of the Church of Ireland in the Irish Church Temporalities Act, which responded to, but did not settle, the tithe issue. Although O'Connell was dismayed by much of the detail of the Church legislation, it did put down an important marker for the future disendowment of the Church of Ireland. Still, he had little to show for his policy of cooperation with the Whigs, and it appears to have been a combination of this sense of disillusionment and pressure from his more radical repeal followers which convinced him that he should abandon his cautious approach to repeal and take the issue to Parliament. Accordingly, in April 1834, O'Connell raised the repeal question in the House of Commons, and he must have been disappointed, but not surprised, at the scale of defeat, as the measure was rejected by 523 votes to 38. Clearly, unlike emancipation, there was no support whatsoever for repeal from any section of the two great parties at Westminster, and it must have been galling for O'Connell to be reminded that there was a clear majority of Irish MPs opposed to repeal.

O'Connell knew enough about political feeling at Westminster to expect a crushing defeat, but such a reverse probably suited his purpose at this stage. He had delayed bringing the repeal issue before Parliament until 1834, and it appears he had done so only reluctantly, following demands from his more headstrong supporters. O'Connell's immediate reaction to the rejection of repeal was to raise the issue in Ireland, as he decided to make repeal the focus of his 1835 general election campaign. Thereafter, however, he virtually abandoned the demand for repeal between 1835 and 1840. The scale of the anti-tithe agitation had highlighted serious problems in channelling popular discontent in Ireland during this period, and this encouraged O'Connell to seek closer cooperation with the Whig party. This development resulted in the Lichfield House compact, an informal alliance between the O'Connellites and the Whigs which was agreed in March 1835. The immediate result was an agreement to combine their voting strength in the House of Commons in order to remove Peel's short-lived administration. While there was no written agreement, the O'Connellites gave their full support to the new Whig government under Lord Melbourne in return for the promise of reform in a number of specified areas. While O'Connell never abandoned his personal commitment to repeal, he was clearly pragmatic enough to give the Lichfield House compact the opportunity to see what benefits the Union could belatedly bring to Ireland. If the Whig alliance did not produce the expected improvements, then O'Connell would be free to revive the repeal agitation in Ireland.

In terms of the legislative record, the results of the Lichfield House compact were extremely disappointing. In 1838 a Tithe Rent Charge Act was passed which reduced tithe payments, wrote off the arrears that had accumulated since 1834 and altered the way in which the tithe was assessed and collected. While this did not abolish tithes, it did enough to ensure that the tithe issue ceased to be a source of popular discontent. Another piece of legislation also focused on the question of poverty in Ireland. The 1838 Poor Relief (Ireland) Act extended the English poor law system to Ireland, but this English solution to an Irish problem did not prove effective. The population explosion in Ireland, and the consequent pressure on resources, had finally forced the government to consider some form of provision for the relief of poverty, but the inadequacy of the response was quickly exposed by the famine.

The new poor law system was based on the workhouse, which was to be established in each of the 130 poor law districts and run by boards of guardians using money collected from local ratepayers. While a system which focused on the provision of employment through relief schemes during the summer period, the 'hungry months' when the previous year's potato harvest had been consumed, would have been more suitable to Irish conditions, no alternative scheme could have coped with the famine. O'Connell himself was dismayed by the poor law system which was established, and he actually voted against the measure, principally, it appears, because he thought that it would impose too heavy a financial burden on the country's property owners.

The final important element of Whig legislation dealt with municipal reform in Ireland. The 1840 Municipal Corporations Act also fell far short of Irish expectations, as many of the proposals made by O'Connell were ignored. The powers given to local councils under the act were not as extensive as those granted in England, and the local government franchise was confined to £10 householders, again more restrictive than on the mainland. While the reorganisation of local government in Ireland enabled O'Connell to become Lord Mayor of Dublin in 1841, the changes were disappointing, and the legislation only served to remind O'Connell that Ireland was denied equal treatment. Clearly, neither the Whig alliance nor the Union itself was working.

Still, the alliance with the Whigs had produced positive results in other ways. The appointment of Thomas Drummond as Under-Secretary in 1835, a position which gave him control over the whole machinery of government based at Dublin Castle, was the key development of the decade for the governing of Ireland. With the support of the Lord Lieutenant, Lord Mulgrave, and the Chief Secretary for Ireland, Viscount Morpeth, Drummond began a root and branch overhaul of the Irish administration. Sympathetic to the plight of the peasantry, he scarcely hid his contempt for the Ascendancy class, believing that it was the attitude of the landowners which was responsible for most of the agrarian unrest in Ireland. Drummond also orchestrated, much to O'Connell's delight, an unrelenting campaign against the Orange Order, which opened the door to the selection of Catholic and liberal Protestant candidates for public appointments. Indeed, O'Connell was not slow in recommending deserving Catholics for many of these appointments. Of greater significance for ordinary Catholics, however, was Drummond's reform of policing which produced a more acceptable service, and Catholics were encouraged to put themselves forward for recruitment to the new police force, with a number being allocated senior positions. Drummond also edged the justice system away from Ascendancy control, and a few Catholics actually became judges. These changes were, in reality, the fruits of the victory in 1829, but they had great symbolic importance, even though only a small section of the Catholic middle class was to benefit financially. Drummond's reforms also created a much better atmosphere in Ireland, and this encouraged O'Connell to consider dropping his demand for repeal altogether, as it appeared that a more enlightened administration could deliver justice to Ireland. Still, this more effective working of the Union could not obscure the Whig government's poor legislative response to Irish needs. The strength and determination of the Conservative opposition ably led by Peel and the massed Tory ranks in the House of Lords both proved major obstacles, but there was always the suspicion that governments at Westminster, even sympathetic ones, had higher priorities than Ireland. Drummond had made a difference, but his death in 1840 was a serious blow to the O'Connellites. When the Melbourne government fell in the following year and the Conservatives took office under Peel, O'Connell was forced to review his strategy. The result was the renewal of the repeal agitation.

In fact, O'Connell was considering such a change in direction before Peel's accession to the premiership. In July 1840 he had launched the Loyal National Repeal Association, and it had been preceded by similar organisations in 1838 and 1839, developments which would suggest that O'Connell had become disillusioned with the outcome of the Whig alliance and was preparing for a return of the Tories. Perhaps surprisingly, the repeal agitation was slow to get off the ground, demonstrating that O'Connell could not turn on and off the agitation as he pleased. More evidence of this apathy arrived in the general election of 1841, when only 18 Repealers were returned. With O'Connell devoting much of his time to his duties as Lord Mayor of Dublin, repeal looked to be an issue which would not fire the enthusiasm of the masses. Two developments transformed the situation. Firstly, a poor harvest in 1842 caused economic distress which quickly manifested itself in a new wave of popular discontent. At the same time, this situation was exploited by a group of radical, younger nationalists who had been attracted to the repeal movement. In October 1842 they produced the first edition of a new newspaper, the *Nation*, which they used to promote the campaign for repeal. The immediate impact of the *Nation*, which achieved circulation figures of 10,000 but enjoyed a readership of 250,000, principally through the use of the repeal reading rooms, quickly generated momentum for the repeal agitation. The key figures who founded the newspaper were Thomas Davis, a Protestant lawyer, Charles Gavan Duffy, a northern Catholic with experience in journalism, and John Blake Dillon, a Catholic from a well known Mayo business family and, like Davis, a graduate of Trinity College. These three were quickly joined by similar youthful, middle class intellectuals from both Catholic and Protestant backgrounds. They later became known as the 'Young Ireland' group.

Although serious differences later emerged between O'Connell and these Young Irelanders, they were, initially, fully behind O'Connell's repeal campaign. The *Nation*'s efforts to create a feeling of nationhood, and its general promotion of the nationalist cause, helped to rally the people, and O'Connell stood ready to spearhead the campaign which, after a few false starts, was now fully under way. In January 1843 he declared that this would be 'repeal year', and the vast audiences which turned out to hear him reinforced his belief that the British government would capitulate, as it did in 1829, under the weight of popular opinion. Indeed, though not all of the Catholic hierarchy embraced repeal as they had emancipation, the two campaigns were remarkably similar. Repeal agitation was very much Catholic in character, and the lower clergy played a crucial organising role at local level. Again, money poured in, allowing O'Connell both to finance an impressive campaign of agitation and to meet his own considerable expenses. But the most abiding memory of the repeal agitation was the 'monster meeting' which attracted huge crowds anxious to hear O'Connell's brilliant denunciation of English misgovernment in Ireland. Between March and October 1843 there were approximately 40 such meetings, usually held on Sundays, drawing crowds frequently in excess of 100,000. The sites chosen for these demonstrations were famous historic locations, and this added to the excitement and sense of occasion generated by O'Connell's stirring oratory.

In terms of organisation and efficiency, and as a means of expressing popular opinion, these gatherings were phenomenal by mid-nineteenth century European standards. O'Connell revelled in the display of patriotism evident in these monster meetings, a development which was carefully nurtured in the pages of the *Nation*. Yet, as before, he refused to be drawn on precisely what he meant by repeal. The re-establishment of Grattan's Parliament was anticipated, but O'Connell preferred to rely on rhetoric and symbols rather than explain how a new constitutional arrangement would work. His speeches during the summer of 1843 were full of defiant messages for the government at Westminster. There were frequent references to past wrongs done to Ireland and, on a number of occasions, there were warnings of dire consequences if the government refused to give way. While these warnings were balanced by repeated declarations that the goal of repeal would be pursued by exclusively peaceful means, it was the possibility of serious violence which concentrated Peel's mind. Occasionally, the demonstrations appeared to be military in character, with large numbers marching in drill formation, while others on horseback, the 'repeal cavalry', were given prominent positions. Certainly, O'Connell wanted to raise the stakes in his desire to force a climb down on the government's part, but it was also the case that most people in the vast crowds, whatever O'Connell's genuine personal assertions of loyalty to the Crown, were anti-English and welcomed the threatening language used by the 'Liberator', as he was known at this time. In June 1843 he issued his famous 'Mallow defiance' which, rather ambiguously, suggested that Irishmen might yet have to fight to win their freedom. Despite such provocative and intemperate language, there is no doubt that O'Connell himself was absolutely opposed to violence, and that he never envisaged reaching a stage which required the use of any kind of unconstitutional action on the part of the repeal movement. His real purpose was to use the monster meetings to show the government that public opinion was clearly behind him, but, if the government saw these demonstrations as a form of intimidation, O'Connell believed that it would only add to the desired effect.

In an attempt to recreate the successful formula which had brought success in 1829, O'Connell sought significant Protestant support for repeal. This was never forthcoming, because Protestant opinion was largely against repeal, though the Protestant element within the Young Ireland group was, of course, an exception. Whatever O'Connell's hopes for broad-based support for repeal agitation, his widely publicised speeches at these great gatherings convinced onlookers that O'Connell was fighting for the Irish nation which, by implication, meant the Catholic nation. Again, economic grievances played their part in this revival of mass politics. Although the *Nation* concentrated on the development of Irish national consciousness, it ran occasional articles demanding land reform, arguing, in particular, that fixity of tenure should be given legal protection. For O'Connell, the solution to all economic problems was the simple one of repeal, and it was only in 1845–46 that he outlined a coherent economic programme which saw him accept the need for a large-scale reform of the land system in Ireland. Still, even then, his economic thinking was governed by the desire to keep state intervention to a minimum, and by his faith in the landowning class.

In 1843, however, he concentrated on the historical grievances under which the Catholic population continued to labour, while cataloguing the failures of the Union. Naturally, such rhetoric sparked concern among Protestants living in Ulster, where it appeared that the Catholic nation was demanding a Catholic state. Indeed, in January 1841, when O'Connell had attempted to raise support for repeal in Belfast, he ran into a storm of opposition. Equally, his strident demands for repeal and the scale of the unparalleled demonstrations in 1843 had forced the Peel administration at Westminster to formulate its response to this new development in Irish nationalism. In 1829 it had bowed to the inevitable and conceded emancipation, but its opposition to repeal was fundamental. O'Connell, for his part, appears to have underestimated Peel's determination to stand by the Union, and he continued to raise the stakes in his attempt to break the government's resolve when, in truth, there was no prospect of success. A clash was unavoidable and it came in October 1843. O'Connell's intention was to hold the last of the 1843 series of monster meetings at Clontarf, just outside Dublin. It was planned that this demonstration would be even more impressive than the others, the culmination of a year's campaigning, and preparations to this effect were well under way when the government decided to ban the meeting. Since the beginning of the repeal agitation, Peel had adopted a cautious approach and had rejected calls for coercion. By October 1843, however, he had decided on a definite course of action. The notices for the Clontarf meeting indicated that it would be more military in character than those that had preceded it, and this gave the government the excuse to issue the proclamation banning it. The Clontarf area was immediately flooded with large numbers of troops to uphold the ban and, fearing bloodshed, O'Connell responded by cancelling the meeting. Such action was in keeping with O'Connell's consistent claims that he would only act constitutionally, but it exposed his earlier words of defiance and threatening language as mere rhetoric. His reputation had taken a blow, but this was partly cushioned by the government's decision to prosecute him for conspiring to cause disaffection. He was jailed in May 1844 but released in September when the House of Lords quashed the sentence on appeal. On his release, the repeal agitation was revived and further demonstrations were organised, but the crusading zeal of 1843 was never recaptured. Unlike emancipation, the repeal campaign would not end in success, because the government led by Peel, which was in a much stronger position than the Wellington administration in 1829, was determined to do everything in its power to prevent it.

Although he had failed in his bid to deliver repeal, O'Connell had a made a powerful and lasting contribution to Irish nationalism. Clearly influenced by British liberal thinking, he had politicised the masses, demonstrated the power of public opinion, achieved success in electoral politics, and established firm links with one of the two great parties at Westminster. Under his leadership the bonds between constitutional nationalism and Catholicism were cemented, a process which undoubtedly promoted sectarianism in Ireland, but O'Connell was more a product of sectarianism than a cause. Of course, without the involvement of the Catholic Church, neither electoral success nor agitation on such a grand scale would have been possible, though it should be recognised that special circumstances were necessary for the mobilisation of the masses. In return, O'Connell supplied the leadership and discipline which ensured that nationalism would not develop as a challenge to the Catholic Church in Ireland. A high rate of literacy was also a necessary prerequisite for a successful mass movement because, without it, the *Nation* would not have enjoyed such influence. O'Connell understood that the driving forces behind the growth of Irish nationalism in this period were both religious and economic. The Catholic middle classes who were prominent in both the emancipation and repeal campaigns believed that they were suffering under discrimination and, though their position began to improve in the 1830s, this only raised expectations even higher. Although O'Connell enjoyed widespread support during specific periods in the 1830s and 1840s, it was among the more bourgeois elements, both in rural and urban Ireland, that his appeal struck the loudest chord. Similarly, whatever the reality, nationalists believed that the Union had stunted Ireland's expected economic growth, a perception which was compounded by the spectacular economic growth being recorded in contemporary Britain.

While he had not delivered repeal, O'Connell had added substance to the view that the Union was the primary cause of Ireland's problems. Like future nationalist leaders, O'Connell had little understanding of Ulster and he failed to make any real impact in the province. Here, both the religious and economic motors driving constitutional nationalism were largely missing. There were, moreover, other regional variations. Nationalism was strongest in Leinster and Munster, particularly in urban areas where, of course, economic expectations were higher. In spite of the difficulties which he faced, O'Connell had introduced the mass of the Irish people to the new idea of democracy and made constitutional nationalism the dominant force in Irish politics, while his influence was felt far beyond Ireland. In the process, he had made Catholics aware of their numerical strength and reminded Protestants of their numerical weakness. O'Connell saw no contradiction between his burning Irish patriotism and his unswerving loyalty to the Crown, and this provided a powerful example for later nationalists in the Home Rule struggle. It was his commitment to constitutionalism that explained his decision to back down in the face of Peel's threat over Clontarf. While O'Connell's climb down later drew fierce criticism from a small minority of militant nationalists, his decision was based on a clear principle and, though the repeal agitation lost momentum and O'Connell's reputation was damaged, constitutional nationalism survived the setback. Moreover, later generations of Irish nationalists recognised that O'Connell was at his most effective when he combined militant rhetoric with practical politics and, therefore, the lines between constitutional and violent nationalism sometimes became blurred.

In responding to the challenge of O'Connellism, Peel did not confine his policy to cracking down on repeal agitation. He had called O'Connell's bluff at Clontarf, but he intended to follow this display of force with a programme of reform which might erode O'Connell's support base and reconcile Irish Catholics to the Union. In 1844 Peel established a Board of Charitable Bequests, on which Catholics were represented, to facilitate donations to the Catholic Church and, in the following year, he increased the annual grant to the Maynooth seminary from £9,000 to £26,000 and made a generous one-off payment of £30,000 for building and repairs. The most significant attempt at conciliation, however, was the 1845 Irish University Act which proposed the establishment of three Queen's Colleges, in Cork, Galway and Belfast, but Peel's higher education offer ran into fierce opposition from O'Connell and the Catholic hierarchy, who feared that it would threaten the Church's influence on the fundamental issue of education. O'Connell's reaction to the university question immediately created a rift within the repeal movement. The Young Ireland group, particularly Davis, had welcomed Peel's initiative, seeing it as a progressive move which would promote unity among the different denominations or, more particularly, among the educated elite which they represented.

Peel's reforms had the effect of releasing tensions which already existed within Irish nationalism. The Young Ireland group, with a strong Protestant representation among its leadership, favoured a nationalism which was inclusive, in addition to one which had solid cultural foundations.

Naturally, this drew the Young Irelanders into conflict with O'Connell. They had clashed over the university question, but Davis's death in September 1845 had created a temporary respite. Nonetheless, O'Connell was unhappy that his authority had been challenged, and he moved to expel the Young Irelanders from the Repeal Association in July 1846, declaring, without any real justification, that they were unwilling to commit themselves to exclusively constitutional methods. Significantly, the Young Irelanders had endorsed the Clontarf decision, but they were critical of O'Connell's more conciliatory stance on his release from prison in September 1844, and their criticism increased with O'Connell's moves to reactivate the Whig alliance towards the end of 1845. With differences in practical politics now added to obvious differences in ideology, a split was inevitable. When it came, both parties were damaged. O'Connell lost the vitality and spirit provided by the Young Ireland intellectuals who, in turn, lost the means of exerting their influence. Only ever a small minority within the Repeal Association, the Young Irelanders faced difficulties in establishing a new organisation able to promote their vision of a more romantic, cultural nationalism. O'Connell's health was now failing, and his powers of judgement were clearly on the wane, but even an O'Connell at the height of his powers would have struggled to maintain the momentum of constitutional nationalism against the background of the famine. By the time of his death in May 1847 constitutional nationalism was irrelevant, but O'Connell had established a secure enough foundation to ensure that it would return as a powerful force given the right circumstances.

3

The Development of Revolutionary Nationalism

ALTHOUGH O'CONNELL CLAIMED to have exposed the Young Ireland movement's ambivalent attitude towards political violence, it was impossible to envisage these idealistic romantic nationalists engaging in rebellion. Nevertheless, excited by examples of revolution in Europe in 1848 and stung into action by the horrors of the famine, a number of these Young Irelanders stumbled into a confused and futile insurrection. Like the two earlier examples of armed revolution, the 1848 uprising proved a hopeless failure but, taken together, these rebellions established a revolutionary tradition in Irish nationalism and provided an inspiration to later generations of violent nationalists. The 1798 rebellion had been on a much bigger scale and it marked the birth of revolutionary nationalism. The participants in 1798 had sought to establish an independent republic by force of arms, but the insurrection was very badly coordinated and local grievances often acted as a stimulus for rebellion. Two other factors present in 1798 also influenced the course of Irish nationalism. Firstly, the rising had grown out of a form of nationalism which could be described as constitutional separatism, and violence was only contemplated as a last, and hopeless, resort when more conventional political avenues had been closed. Secondly, in spite of heavy northern Presbyterian participation, there were obvious sectarian motives at work in 1798 and, consequently, revolutionary nationalism developed a strong sectarian character in Irish Protestant eyes.

In many ways, the 1803 insurrection led by Robert Emmet was a direct result of the 1798 rebellion. Expelled from Trinity College for his radical views, the young Emmet spent two years in France attempting to secure further military support for a fresh uprising. When this proved unsuccessful, he returned to Ireland and soon engaged with other veterans of 1798 in the planning of a new rising, somehow emerging as the leading conspirator. His plan was to seize Dublin Castle and other important buildings in the capital, a move which, he hoped, would spark a more widespread rebellion in the country at large. What followed, on Saturday 23 July 1803, was a confusing episode, bordering on chaotic farce, as approximately 300 men took to the streets of Dublin. The military planning was thoroughly inadequate and, with such a small force of untrained men at his command, Emmet, who proved a hesitant commander, chose not to attack Dublin Castle, his original target. The small force had occupied two streets when troops arrived and quickly dispersed the insurgents. Emmet fled to County Wicklow, but was captured in the following month and executed on 20 September. The rising, more a fracas than a rebellion, had been a catastrophic military failure and it finished the attempts of the remaining United Irish conspirators to plan a further rising. The number of insurgents had been shockingly low and no spontaneous rising had followed in the rest of the country, but, in spite of the abject failure of the 1803 uprising, it made an important contribution to revolutionary nationalism in Ireland. In his dramatic plea from the dock, Emmet demanded that his epitaph should only be written when Ireland had won her freedom from Britain. This symbolic gesture provided a powerful inspiration for later generations of nationalists, and what might have been remembered as an embarrassing failure was transformed into a heroic act of patriotism which became embedded in the ideology of militant republicanism. In fact, failure itself became a triumph, as the hopelessness of the entire venture, allied to Emmet's youthful, almost innocent, idealism, made the 1803 debacle more attractive to future groups of violent nationalists.

Despite its legacy, it would be wrong to place too much importance on events such as the 1803 rebellion. Violent nationalism surfaced only sporadically and, on such occasions, it was characterised by a lack of popular support. Indeed, even the idea of a tradition of revolutionary nationalism appears misleading. Ireland did not have such a tradition of violent nationalism, but it did have a tradition of violence in rural society. Sometimes this was due to vague notions of nationalism, but, more frequently, agrarian unrest was a consequence of local economic grievances. The first half of the nineteenth century witnessed the rapid growth of a host of agrarian secret societies which, as they did during the anti-tithe protests in the 1830s, spread chaos in rural Ireland and forced the government to respond with coercive legislation. Nationalism, or even politics, was never the motive for such activities, but clashes with the authorities could easily develop a political dimension. Of these secret societies, the Ribbon organisation was easily the most political in character. It also had an urban base, recruiting among the Dublin artisan class, but its members were drawn from most areas of the country. The Ribbonmen had their origins in the Defender tradition of the late eighteenth century and, as such, they were openly sectarian, while adhering to a vague concept of revolutionary nationalism. Yet, while the sporadic violence perpetrated by all of these secret societies became part of the culture of rural society, the link between their activities and violent nationalism was, at best, tenuous. During certain times, however, particularly in the late 1820s and early 1840s, O'Connell's militant rhetoric and programme of direct action must have appealed to all shades of militant nationalism, including the various secret societies, thereby demonstrating that there could be considerable overlap between constitutional and revolutionary nationalism. Indeed, during the 1840s, the Young Irelanders made a significant contribution to all three forms of nationalism – constitutional, revolutionary and cultural.

In January 1847 the Young Irelanders who had split with O'Connell formed the Irish Confederation, but it was almost a year before the new body issued a programme outlining its principles. Most importantly, this proclaimed Ireland's right to self-government and reaffirmed a commitment to non-violent methods, thus following closely the original policy of the Repeal Association, but these lofty political aspirations were irrelevant to an Ireland gripped by famine. The most prominent member of the Irish Confederation was William Smith O'Brien, a liberal in politics from a Protestant gentry background. An MP since 1828, Smith O'Brien had supported emancipation before being persuaded that repeal of the Union was the only solution to Ireland's problems. Of course, Smith O'Brien was exactly the type of high profile convert, a liberal Protestant with aristocratic connections, that O'Connell was seeking, and he was quickly elevated to the top rank of the Repeal Association which he joined in 1843, serving as leader during O'Connell's term of imprisonment in 1844. Later, Smith O'Brien attempted to heal the divisions between O'Connell and the Young Irelanders but, when the Liberator forced the issue, Smith O'Brien departed with the Young Ireland group to form the Irish Confederation. If the famine sidelined the lofty, idealistic version of Irish nationalism preached by Smith O'Brien, it also encouraged more extreme nationalists on the fringe of the Young Ireland movement who believed that the upheaval in Irish society caused by the agrarian crisis demanded action, and not more political theorising.

Among those who argued that the repeal aim should be abandoned in favour of direct action to save the tenant farming class was James Fintan Lalor. A hitherto obscure figure, who had become associated with the Irish Confederation in 1847, Lalor publicised a programme for agrarian revolution in a number of open letters to the *Nation*. Lalor's proposals involved concerted action by Ireland's tenant farmers, who would refuse to pay rents until the landlords accepted the principle of co-ownership between landlord and tenant. While he was not against the idea of the peasantry imposing their will through force of arms, he argued that his idea of 'moral insurrection' was more suited to contemporary circumstances and claimed that the famine had already done a great deal to undermine the old land system. Though the famine had, in fact, rendered the possibility of such direct action even less likely, Lalor had made a valuable contribution to Irish nationalism by linking it to the struggle between landlord and tenant. While he failed to persuade the Irish Confederation to support his initiative, Lalor managed to convince a leading member, John Mitchel, that by coupling the land issue and the national question, it opened up the prospect of success for revolutionary nationalism. Mitchel, the son of a Unitarian minister from Ulster, was becoming increasingly frustrated by the Confederation's inability to produce a coherent programme of its own to respond to the challenge of the famine, and, by the end of 1847, he was convinced that only prompt revolutionary action in the form of a peasant-led rebellion could rescue the situation. Withdrawing from the Irish Confederation, Mitchel established a new newspaper, the *United Irishman*, and called for an immediate insurrection. With a number of militant nationalists beginning to side with Mitchel, Smith O'Brien, the senior figure in the Young Ireland movement, tried to hold the line, arguing that only constitutional action should be contemplated and hoping that the landlord class would back his renewed call for the repeal of the Union.

Although Smith O'Brien had openly rejected Mitchel's

violent radicalism, the stunning success of French revolutionaries in February 1848 had caused Young Irelanders, who had consistently looked to nationalist movements in Europe for inspiration, to reassess Mitchel's extremist programme. Subsequently, the euphoria created by events on the continent, and the increasing sense of desperation caused by the experience of famine, caused the former moderates within the Young Ireland movement to consider the prospects for an Irish revolution. The government was aware of these developments and Mitchel, Smith O'Brien and Thomas Francis Meagher, another militant who had earlier led the Young Ireland attack on O'Connell, were arrested in the spring of 1848. Brought to trial in May, Meagher and Smith O'Brien were released amid scenes of great celebration, but Mitchel was found guilty of treason-felony, a new offence introduced only weeks earlier, and transported. Escaping from Tasmania to America in 1853, Mitchel became involved in Irish-American politics, and his famous *Jail Journal*, which was to have a powerful impact on later nationalist thinking, was published in 1854. In 1875 he returned to Ireland and immediately became involved in politics, winning the Westminster seat of County Tipperary shortly before his death, a victory which was partly attributable to Mitchel's martyr status following his transportation to Australia. Later, the cautious Smith O'Brien returned to his Limerick estate, but, in July, he decided to tour the country in an attempt to gauge the level of support for revolution. Before this task had been completed, however, the government again moved quickly to arrest prominent figures, including Meagher and Gavan Duffy. This had been made possible by emergency legislation, temporarily suspending habeas corpus, which had been rushed through Parliament in July. Smith O'Brien was still dithering about the prospects for a rebellion when the arrests were made, and he was now faced with the choice of fleeing from arrest or launching an insurrection. While he was extremely nervous about committing his followers to a rebellion, he became convinced, following urgent discussions with Meagher and John Blake Dillon, that their honour would only be saved by taking up arms.

Smith O'Brien was a reluctant and unlikely revolutionary leader. He had only committed himself to revolution when the government had arrested leading Young Ireland militants and banned the Confederate Clubs that had sprung up in the summer of 1847. Together with Meagher and Dillon, Smith O'Brien sought to rally the peasantry in the south of the country, a demoralising venture at a time when the rural poor were obviously more concerned with survival. By 29 July 1848, Smith O'Brien and about 50 followers had congregated near Ballingarry, County Tipperary, and a confrontation ensued between the small band of Young Ireland rebels and members of the Irish Constabulary. In what became known as the 'battle of the Widow McCormack's cabbage patch', armed police, who had taken refuge in Mrs McCormack's house, easily dispersed the insurgents. Smith O'Brien had proved himself an ineffective leader of a hopelessly disorganised rebellion, and he was arrested as he made his way back to County Limerick. Along with other leading figures who had been arrested, Smith O'Brien was convicted of high treason and transported to Tasmania. A number of younger insurgents evaded the authorities and some, notably James Stephens and John O'Mahony, escaped to France where they engaged with fellow revolutionaries and provided a direct link between the Young Ireland rebels and the subsequent Fenian movement. The timing of the insurrection was suicidal, as the famine ensured that the rebellion would not enjoy any degree of popular support. Like 1803, the tiny number of committed revolutionaries was illuminating but, in spite of this, the 1848 rising took its place in the sequence of unsuccessful rebellions and served both as an inspiration and an example to future generations of revolutionary nationalists. Yet its main legacy was not the unmitigated military fiasco but its contribution to the development of a greater sense of nationality among the politically conscious. In the process, these expressions of cultural nationalism were given a sharp political edge.

While the famine guaranteed the failure of the Young Ireland rising, it also had a major impact on the future course of Irish nationalism. The scale of the suffering and the Westminster government's inadequate and callous response to the catastrophe were ingrained in the Irish national psyche. It did not, however, create anti-English sentiment. This already existed and had, of course, been exploited by O'Connell, but the famine undoubtedly deepened anti-English feeling and gave it a more precise *raison d'etre*. The famine also produced a huge diaspora, and it was among this body that Mitchel's later writings, which charged the British government with genocide, received most attention. Consequently, the quest for vengeance exerted a powerful influence among Irish-Americans, and this was subsequently translated into support for violent nationalism. In Ireland, moreover, the memory of the famine was regularly used by both constitutional and revolutionary nationalists in their attempts to mobilise support. In this development Lalor's writings continued to reach a wide audience. His views had motivated Young Ireland insurgents and, more than any other writer of the Young Ireland era, Lalor had forged an unbreakable link between the land and the national questions which provided the basis for the advance of nationalist thinking in the Parnellite period. Indeed, it was this merger of economic and political forces which gave nationalism a new vitality in the second half of the nineteenth century.

Yet the famine did not produce an immediate boost for Irish nationalism. It ended mass agitation for repeal and, though the land question had become a central issue in Irish politics, it was to be some time before a new movement with significant popular support emerged. One difficulty was the creation of a nationwide organisation which would enjoy sustainable, long-term support from the various local concerns and grievances present in the immediate post-famine period. Some attempt to respond to this problem was made in August 1850 when the Irish Tenant League was formed to protect tenant interests. Specifically, the new organisation was established to campaign for the 'three Fs': fair rents, which would be independently fixed; fixity of tenure, which would prevent evictions so long as a tenant paid his rent; and free sale, which would allow a tenant to be compensated for improvements he had made to his holding. This Irish Tenant League had grown out of the great agrarian crisis, as those farmers who had survived the famine were faced with weak agricultural prices and the growing threat of eviction, and the intention was to build up an independent parliamentary party which would fight for tenant protection at Westminster. Further encouragement was offered by the 1850 Irish Franchise Act, which more than doubled the electorate, and, following the general election of 1852, 48 MPs took a pledge to act independently and oppose any government that refused concessions to Ireland on the land question. This Independent Opposition party demonstrated its potential in December 1852, when it helped to topple the minority Conservative government, but it lacked any real discipline and was quickly torn apart by internal bickering. The rapid demise of the Independent Opposition party ended the possibility of concerted political action aimed at redressing particular agrarian grievances, but it was the steady recovery in agricultural prices which sharply reduced the level of tenant agitation.

Significantly, this setback for constitutional politics in the late 1850s coincided with the growth of a much more militant form of nationalism. The Fenian movement was also a direct consequence of the 1848 rising. It was founded by some of the 1848 participants who were determined to erase the memory of the Young Ireland rebellion and present a more formidable challenge to British rule in Ireland. The key figures were James Stephens and John O'Mahony, both of whom had fled to Paris following the collapse of the rising. Here they came under the influence of revolutionary societies on the continent and this persuaded them to consider the establishment of a centrally directed, oath-bound secret society which would be based on the cell structure to safeguard internal security. Stephens had returned to Ireland in 1856 and was soon in contact with radical political elements, particularly in the south-west of the country. At the end of 1853, O'Mahony had left Paris for America where he sought to channel bitterness towards England into support for revolutionary action in Ireland. With encouragement from O'Mahony and guarantees of Irish-American support, Stephens founded the Irish Republican Brotherhood (IRB), though the term Fenians was more commonly used, and immediately began the task of swearing in members. While the new movement built on the secret society tradition in Ireland, the Fenians articulated a clear political goal in their desire to establish an independent Irish republic. There was also a rejection of constitutionalism and a commitment to the use of violence to achieve this goal, together with an understanding that the Fenian movement had to be ready to seize any opportunity which presented itself.

The Fenian movement was non-sectarian and anti-clerical. It claimed a direct link with the United Irishmen and subscribed to Davis's vision of an inclusive nationalism, but it never attracted anything like a significant number of Protestants and failed to develop a following among Ulster Presbyterians. The movement also faced fierce opposition from the Catholic Church which had always been hostile to Catholics joining any secret, oath-bound organisation. Much of this opposition emanated from Paul Cullen, the Archbishop of Dublin, who regarded Fenianism as a direct challenge to the Church's authority and viewed revolutionary activity as an attack on religion. Yet, in spite of such powerful clerical opposition, the Fenian movement was beginning to expand. It was strongest in urban centres where it attracted support among the artisans and petty bourgeoisie. These craftsmen, clerks, teachers and shop assistants were independently-minded people, for whom advancement, either political or social, was problematic. Many of these new recruits were their own masters and they had the time to indulge in an organisation whose secrecy and rituals offered the potential for the occasional exciting evening in what was, otherwise, a fairly dreary existence. Indeed, in many towns the Fenian movement played a prominent role in the organisation of a variety of social and recreational pastimes, and this aspect alone may have been sufficient to attract interested members. Where it made inroads in rural Ireland, the Fenians made most appeal to the poorer tenant farmers and the landless labourers. Taking their cue from Lalor, the Fenians repeated the slogan 'the land for the people', striking a chord in selected areas where Ribbonism had been strong.

Added publicity for the Fenian movement came with the carefully staged funeral of Terence Bellew MacManus, a Young Ireland veteran who died in San Francisco in 1861. American Fenians decided to exhume the body and ship it back to Dublin where a public row broke out between Archbishop Cullen and the MacManus Committee, the Fenian front organisation with responsibility for coordinating the event in Ireland. Seeing the entire episode as a Fenian publicity stunt, Cullen refused to allow the body to lie in state in Dublin's Pro-Cathedral, and a stand off between the Fenians and the Church ensued. However, Cullen was defied when Father Lavelle, a priest with strong Fenian sympathies, performed the religious duties at the funeral. In fact, the whole affair caught the public's imagination and a huge crowd lined the funeral route to Glasnevin. The MacManus episode demonstrated that Fenianism could overcome clerical opposition. This was confirmed with the launch of the National Association in 1864. Backed by Cullen and most of the hierarchy, the National Association was a moderate constitutional nationalist body built on O'Connellite principles, but under tight clerical control. Yet it had very little impact on Irish society and failed to halt the spread of Fenianism. By the mid-1860s the Fenian movement had 50,000 members, though Fenian claims frequently exaggerated this figure, and it was undoubtedly successful in rekindling political activity in many areas of the country following the collapse of O'Connellism and the upheaval of the famine. In achieving this success, Fenianism was able to respond to structural changes in post-famine society and managed to articulate the feelings and frustrations of the petty bourgeois elements which dominated the movement. Through the *Irish People*, founded in 1863, the movement openly touted for new recruits, while publicising its revolutionary ideas and demanding that the Church stay out of politics.

Not surprisingly, the movement's propaganda impact and its success in attracting new recruits drew it to the attention of the government which had, hitherto, adopted a low-key attitude to Fenian activities. In September 1865 the government finally acted by suppressing the *Irish People* and arresting Charles Kickham, Thomas Clarke Luby and John O'Leary, the main contributors to the Fenian newspaper. Stephens had escaped arrest, but he hesitated over calling a rebellion. The IRB leadership, and Stephens in particular, had been promising a rebellion, and this was anticipated in 1865 when the organisation appeared ready to engage in revolution. The end of the American Civil War in 1865, in which Irish regiments had played a prominent role, saw the arrival in Ireland of more than 100 soldiers who had fought in the conflict and were now pressing for a rebellion. Still, the arrest of key figures in September had caused confusion, and Stephens himself was in custody by November though, with the aid of Fenian sympathisers, he escaped within a fortnight. Hiding in a Dublin safe house, Stephens, in spite of pleas from his colleagues, still refused to sanction a rebellion. At the same time, the government, through its network of informers, was building up a clear picture of the movement's intentions, and its move to suspend habeas corpus in February 1866 was immediately followed by a wave of arrests which threw Fenianism into disarray. Stephens fled Ireland and arrived in America in May 1866, and here he faced the formidable task of healing a serious internal split in the American branch of the brotherhood. One group wanted to plan an invasion of Canada, but Stephens argued forcefully that American Fenians must support a rising in Ireland which, he promised, would be launched before the end of 1866. By this stage, however, his American lieutenants were becoming disillusioned with Stephens and his private insistence on the postponement of a rebellion until a more suitable moment. This quickly developed into open warfare and, following a series of meetings in New York in December 1866, Stephens was removed from the leadership and replaced by Colonel TJ Kelly, a native of Galway and veteran of the Civil War. Almost immediately, Kelly left America with other civil war veterans. His destination was not Ireland but Britain, where Kelly and his associates assumed that they could conduct final preparations for a rising without interference from the authorities. Arriving in London at the end of January 1867, Kelly learned that Fenian elements among the Irish population in Britain had already drawn up their own plan of action. Problems occurred, however, when an arms raid on Chester Castle in February had to be aborted at the last minute on the discovery that the garrison guarding the castle had been reinforced following a tip-off.

Attention then switched to Ireland where, in Stephens's absence, the brotherhood was determined to launch the long-awaited rebellion. In February, a brief skirmish took place in

County Kerry, and this was followed on the night of 4–5 March by a series of minor risings in Dublin, Tipperary, Cork, Limerick, Clare and Wicklow. The failure to coordinate these actions, the damage caused by informers, severe snow storms and resolute action by government forces all combined to ensure that the rebellion would end in defeat. Mopping up operations continued over the next few weeks, but the Fenian rising of 1867 had caused very little loss of life, thereby confirming that it was more of a gesture by impatient Fenian activists, whose morale had been sapped by repeated postponements, than a serious attempt to drive the British out of Ireland. But the collapse of the rising did not mean the end of the Fenian organisation, which retained considerable support in Ireland, America and Britain. Kelly was still active in England, but he was arrested in Manchester in September after being spotted acting suspiciously in a doorway. One week later, as he was being transported between the jail and the local court, an armed Fenian gang trying to rescue Kelly attacked his carriage. In the ensuing melee an unarmed policeman was shot dead and, following a number of subsequent arrests, three Fenian volunteers were tried for their role in the raid and executed on 24 November 1867. The execution of these 'Manchester Martyrs' stirred passions right across nationalist Ireland. The embarrassing failure of the attempted rebellion was quickly forgotten, as an outpouring of sympathy helped to ensure the survival of Fenianism. The Catholic Church, previously hostile to the organisation, condemned the executions and organised commemorative masses which were held in different parts of Ireland. Fenianism had provided violent nationalism with a new group of martyrs, while adding to the sequence of failed insurrections.

Yet more than previous examples of revolutionary nationalism, Fenianism was strongly identified with the use of physical force. Although the stipulated goal was an Irish republic, it was true that many Fenian activists did not dwell on the precise nature of such a constitutional change, but were really separatist nationalists who simply wanted as much freedom as possible for Ireland. While their movement had been infiltrated by government agents, Fenians themselves were keen to infiltrate other nationalist organisations and influence their direction. Their contribution to the development of a more militant form of nationalism was also enhanced by their association with their American sister organisation, which stood ready to provide the necessary support to make armed insurrection in Ireland a reality. At the heart of the Fenian movement, however, was its commitment to an insurrection planned by revolutionary conspirators. This legacy of revolutionary conspiracy was, of course, most famously revealed in 1916. The activities of the Fenian movement also forced the government to move the Irish question up its list of priorities. This was guaranteed when, in December 1867, an attempt was made to spring an important Fenian activist, Richard Burke, from Clerkenwell prison in London. In an attempt to blast a hole in the prison wall, the Fenian gang killed 20 innocent Londoners. Public opinion in England was outraged, as the atrocity forced the Liberal government of the day to give serious attention to Ireland.

But the impact of Fenianism was also felt outside the narrow confines of revolutionary nationalism. In making contact with like-minded nationalists on his return to Ireland in 1856, Stephens had met members of the Phoenix literary societies. These nationalist clubs, the most famous of which was the Phoenix Society founded in Skibbereen, County Cork, by Jeremiah O'Donovan Rossa, focused on the revival of Gaelic culture, but lively political discussion generated by advanced nationalist thinking was a fundamental part of life in these emerging literary and political groups. The new Fenian organisation soon absorbed the Phoenix Society and this, together with the contribution made by O'Donovan Rossa,

Charles Kickham and other 'literary Fenians' gave the movement a cultural dimension which appealed, in particular, to the petty bourgeoisie. Later, the coexistence of revolutionary and cultural nationalism made a powerful contribution to the 1916 rising. Fenianism also built on the tradition of the agrarian secret society in Ireland and, almost inevitably, the movement was drawn to the land question. While it never produced a coherent social programme, it did subscribe to Lalor's anti-landlord thinking and, in time, this helped to push constitutional and revolutionary nationalism closer together. This process was also made possible by the Fenian movement's growing respectability, something that was partly attributable to the easing of clerical hostility to the organisation. Hard evidence of this came in November 1869, when O'Donovan Rossa won the Tipperary by-election while serving a prison sentence for Fenian activities. The by-election victory demonstrated that constitutional and revolutionary nationalism could work together for a common purpose given the right circumstances, and this laid the foundation for nationalist success in the last quarter of the nineteenth century.

4

Land and Nationalism

THE FOCUS ON THE LAND question highlighted the economic grievance which provided the momentum for Irish nationalism in the last quarter of the nineteenth century. The landlord class was stereotyped as alien, differing in religion and nationality from the vast bulk of the tenant farmers. This enabled the various strata in rural Ireland, ranging from the well off grazier to the landless labourer, to unite against the discredited landlords in the expectation that their action would lead to radical social change based on an overhaul of the land system. By channelling this agrarian discontent into support for a new and more dynamic form of nationalism, the tenant farmers, the largest group in Irish society, were mobilised to fight for economic and political change. In O'Connell's era economic grievances had been a factor in the mobilisation of the peasantry and, in the 1850s, the tenant-right movement had attracted a measure of support by campaigning for the three Fs, but no progress on the land question had been forthcoming. This would change towards the end of the century as a revitalised nationalist movement, resuscitated by land agitation, pressed the case for reform at Westminster. There too, there was some ground for optimism. William Ewart Gladstone, the new Liberal Prime Minister, had, mainly because of the Fenian rising, taken a keen interest in Ireland and was determined to introduce measures which, he hoped, would improve the situation sufficiently to erode support for violent nationalism. In 1869 his Irish Church Act, which disestablished the Church of Ireland, acknowledged Catholic numbers, but it was bitterly opposed by Irish Protestants. His 1870 Land Act, which gave legal recognition to the 'Ulster Custom' by compensating an outgoing tenant for improvements, made little impact, but it was given subsequent symbolic endorsement as it became the first in a celebrated series of land reforms.

In Ireland itself the Amnesty Association, which had been established to campaign for the release of Fenian prisoners, was making more impact. The well known barrister Isaac Butt, who had defended many of the Fenian leaders at their high-profile trials, became president of the Association and, in the late summer of 1869, he organised a series of meetings which rekindled memories of O'Connell. In October a crowd estimated at 200,000 turned out for a rally near Cabra, but these demonstrations were subsequently suspended as the movement's leaders feared the development of another Clontarf. Some success was achieved with the release of a number of minor figures, but the real significance of the Amnesty Association was the collaboration between constitutional nationalists like Butt and the Fenians who were active in the movement. While Butt had understood the motivation of revolutionary nationalists, he was an unequivocal opponent of political violence and sought, therefore, to divert the Fenian movement down a more constitutional route. Stephens had always opposed such a dilution of revolutionary principles, but his removal and subsequent repudiation had opened up the prospect of a more flexible approach by the new leaders. The result was Fenian approval for Butt's Home Government Association, formed in 1870 to promote the cause of a new parliament in Dublin. In 1873 this comfortable, middle class talking shop was dissolved and a new organisation, the Home Rule League, took its place. By this stage the need for more effective organisation had been recognised, and the demand for Home

Rule had aroused interest among a growing number of the Catholic clergy. Moreover, the Fenian movement had added its tentative support to Butt's new venture. Following a decision of the IRB Supreme Council, Butt was informed that the Fenians would play a supporting role for a period of three years in an attempt to win a Home Rule parliament for Ireland. This was a bonus, because it was clear to Butt that the Fenian organisation had aroused national consciousness and given him the opportunity to take advantage of this development. Progress in this direction would also enable Butt to shepherd Fenianism away from violence.

Almost immediately, the Home Rule League was presented with an opportunity to test its support when a general election was called at the beginning of 1874. Butt's efforts were rewarded with the return of 59 Home Rule MPs, but this figure was misleading. At the previous general election the Liberals had been the dominant party in Ireland, winning two-thirds of the country's 105 seats, and a significant number of new Home Rulers, as they became known, were former Liberals who only adopted the Home Rule tag to ensure their return to Parliament. In reality, there were only about 20 who were genuinely committed to the Home Rule cause. Still, Butt had made an impressive beginning, but he was unable to turn this initial electoral success in Ireland to any real advantage at Westminster. When he did attend, Butt was keen to engage in logical and reasoned argument in an attempt to persuade the House of Commons that a devolved scheme of government would bring benefits to both Britain and Ireland. His case, though eloquently delivered, was swiftly rejected by the new Conservative government led by Benjamin Disraeli, and the genteel Butt was content to accept the status quo. In addition, Butt failed to provide the type of strong leadership necessary to hold together the disparate Home Rule group at Westminster and it soon split into a number of disorganised factions. Undoubtedly, his politeness and ineffectiveness undermined Butt's reputation with those Fenians who had been prepared to give constitutionalism a chance. These men were more impressed by the activities of a small group of more militant Home Rulers who refused to be constrained by Butt's moderation. The key activist among the militants was Joseph Biggar, a prosperous Belfast provision merchant, who had been elected MP for Cavan in 1874.

Biggar paid no respect to the niceties of parliamentary politics. From 1875 to 1877 Biggar orchestrated a campaign of 'parliamentary obstruction' in which he and his associates exploited every opportunity to delay business in the House of Commons. Though only a handful of Home Rulers were involved, they could, by carefully coordinating their activities, bring the House to a standstill. Of course, their actions infuriated other MPs and made them extremely unpopular at Westminster, but they did fire popular interest in Ireland. In 1875 Biggar actually joined the Fenian movement and, in the following year, he was elevated to the organisation's ruling body, the IRB Supreme Council, where he joined another MP, John O'Connor Power, who had become MP for Mayo in 1874. Although their refusal to leave Parliament led to the expulsion of both Biggar and O'Connor Power from the Fenian movement in 1877, when the Supreme Council, by a majority of just one vote, suspended its cooperation with the Home Rulers, the actions of these constitutional Fenians had given the Home Rule movement a cutting edge. It was the strategy of parliamentary obstruction which first brought Charles Stewart Parnell to prominence. Parnell was an Anglo-Irish Protestant landlord from County Wicklow who had been returned as an MP for County Meath at a by-election in April 1875. While his family had been active in public life for 100 years, Parnell himself had little political experience and, initially at least, there was little to suggest that he would become the dominant figure in the Home Rule party. From his American mother he had inherited a deep-seated antipathy to

England, and his experiences as an undergraduate at Cambridge reinforced this prejudice. Although he was not a gifted public speaker in the Butt mould, Parnell's social standing gave him a natural self-confidence, and he was dismissive of the formalities at Westminster and never in awe of fellow MPs from a similar social background. Ruffling parliamentary feathers did not perturb Parnell, and his participation in the obstruction campaign raised his profile in Ireland. For Parnell, obstruction was a simple device for creating interest and maintaining morale in Ireland, and the frequent denunciation of Parnell, Biggar and the others achieved his objective. Of course, an embarrassed Butt joined in the criticism of Parnell and the tactic of obstruction. Having had his argument for Home Rule rejected at Westminster, Butt was content to wait on the sideline expecting sympathy from British MPs who could eventually be persuaded of the logic of a Home Rule solution. Parnell was frustrated by this lack of activity and by Butt's apparent lack of enthusiasm for political struggle and, in time, he became a rival for the leadership.

In Ireland, meanwhile, the post-famine era witnessed important changes in rural society. Since the 1850s there had been a marked, if uneven, rise in agricultural prices. The years 1859–64 were difficult but the overall pattern, until the late 1870s, was one of prices nudging ahead of rents. For many tenant farmers, therefore, the post-famine period saw modest improvement and increased prosperity. But such progress was not uniform. After the famine the number of cottiers and landless labourers, as a percentage of the total rural population, declined sharply, allowing the tenant farmers to become a majority. At the same time, a clear trend towards the consolidation of holdings was established, and this meant that the stronger farmers tended to increase both in number and in importance. Further changes occurred with the shift from arable to pastoral farming, a development pushed by the stronger farmers who had some access to capital. Profit was the motivation for this switch to pasture, as the increasing volatility in the price of cereals and the sharp rise in foreign competition made livestock farming more attractive. Yet there were marked regional differences in the overall pattern of development. The move away from tillage and the consolidation of holdings combined to create large grazing 'ranches' in the east and midlands, but these changes made less impact in the west. Although subsistence farming had given way to commercial farming over most of the country, Connacht still had large numbers of cottiers and small farmers who continued to rely on the potato. Yet, even in the west, these smallholdings were interspersed with a number of large ranches, thus creating the conditions for tension between the grazier and small farmer. When this was added to the existing strained relationship between landlord and tenant, rural society in the west was characterised by a complex mix of social tension. Pressure on the land continued to be a feature of rural society in Connacht. While it suffered more during the famine than any other province, Connacht emigration rates only caught up with the national average in 1870, and the rate of population decrease was also much lower in Connacht in the 30 years after the famine, as the move away from the pattern of early marriages was delayed in the west.

It was no surprise, therefore, that the agricultural depression, which began in 1877 and affected the whole country, was most keenly felt in Connacht. A combination of a poor potato crop and a worldwide depression, conditions which prevailed in the following two years, produced the most serious and sustained agricultural depression since the famine. A prolonged period of poor weather exacerbated the deteriorating situation and, by 1879, the prospect of another famine became a reality for many of the west's poorest farmers. At the same time, the slump in cattle prices hit both the smallholder who reared cattle and the grazier who purchased these animals for finishing. Nowhere were these factors more important than in County Mayo, which had a strong tradition of tenant organisation. Livestock farming had become increasingly important in a county where the move to cattle was already under way before the famine. Even poor farmers, whose staple diet remained the potato, could derive some benefit from the cattle boom by raising a few livestock on marginal land and then selling them to the large graziers. Many of the county's graziers were actually shopkeepers, publicans, merchants and professional men from the towns, who rented the best local agricultural land and employed stockmen to look after their livestock interests. Previously, relations between this rural bourgeoisie and the poorer farmers had been difficult, but the agricultural crisis of 1877–79 united these different social groups for a brief period. Spurred on by the threat of mass evictions, the Mayo farming classes came together to challenge the authority of the landlords and demand a reduction in rent. This new wave of economic distress coincided with a rise in agrarian unrest, as an increasingly desperate rural population vented its frustration in the traditional manner. Indeed, the recession was intensified by the sudden drop in demand for seasonal labour in Britain, which had previously offered an outlet for many of the county's poorest families.

The agricultural depression of the late 1870s provided the backdrop to a revival of nationalism which, while drawing on past experience, was new in form because of its direct association with a particular economic grievance. This had the effect of mobilising the tenant farming classes in the struggle against the alien landlords and a foreign government. Mayo provided the starting point, because a large section of the county's tenant farmers had recently been politicised by an energetic group of leaders who were able to coordinate and direct the agrarian agitation. The election team which had run O'Connor Power's campaign in 1874 had been hard at work in spreading radical ideas which pulled together agrarian and political thinking. O'Connor Power embarked on annual lecture tours which raised political consciousness among his new tenant farmer supporters, and his views were repeatedly endorsed in the local press. The local Fenian movement was also active in the O'Connor Power circle, using its influence to radicalise political thinking in the county. It was this energetic and dynamic local leadership which was able to coordinate the agrarian agitation and give it a political dimension.

This was the situation which Michael Davitt found when he toured the county in 1878. Davitt was the son of a Mayo tenant farmer who had been evicted from his holding in 1851. Raised in Lancashire where he lost his right arm in a factory accident in 1857, Davitt joined the Fenian movement in England and was jailed in 1870 for his part in a gun-running plot. On his release from Dartmoor prison in December 1877, he returned to Mayo and toured the county, delivering a series of political speeches in which he outlined the separatist goal. But what struck Davitt on his return was the discovery that the Mayo tenant farmers were so far advanced in their approach to the land issue. Soon, he added his energy and organisational ability to the agrarian movement in Mayo. Indeed, Davitt played some part, though not the key role, in the arrangements for the famous Irishtown meeting in April 1879, which attracted a crowd of about 10,000 eager to adopt resolutions demanding a reduction in rents and the abolition of landlordism.

Parnell did not foresee the agrarian crisis that was to transform the fortunes of the Home Rule party. Indeed, he was slow to respond to the political potential of the agrarian movement in Mayo, rejecting a number of calls to organise an alliance of MPs and land reformers. Although the success of the Irishtown meeting, which he did not attend, warned Parnell that the tenant agitation in Mayo had the capacity to develop a momentum of its own, he still hesitated. In the end, it was the persistent prompting of Michael Davitt that persuaded him to identify with the land issue, and he agreed to attend a second meeting, planned for Westport on 8 June 1879. At the Westport rally Parnell outlined his own views on the land question to another large audience. During the agrarian crisis Parnell had moved tentatively towards Lalor's notion of 'the land for the people', but he was careful to stress that this was a long-term goal. Parnell was firmly opposed to social revolution and he argued for conciliation with the landlords in his demand for a fair rent, which he defined as one that "the tenant can reasonably pay according to the times". Yet Parnell also appealed to the agrarian radicals by declaring that tenants should "keep a firm grip" on their holdings, if they were threatened with eviction. Still, Parnell's call for direct action was deliberately vague, as he neglected to outline the precise steps that tenant farmers should take to defend their position. To some extent, therefore, Parnell was feeling his way on the land question. Although he had hesitated before committing himself, Parnell sensed that the growing agrarian unrest in the west had developed into a major political grievance which he had to direct. Furthermore, the agitation in Mayo had enhanced O'Connor Power's leadership claims over the militant wing of the Home Rule party, and Parnell realised that he had to move decisively in order to outmanoeuvre his rival. One thing Parnell understood perfectly was power. While his quarrel with Butt had made him very unpopular with many of his more cautious parliamentary colleagues, his ambition remained undiminished and he was ruthless in his pursuit of power. Butt had died in May 1879 and the Wicklow landlord was determined to replace him and provide the Home Rule party with much more vigorous and dynamic leadership. In fact, Parnell's path to the leadership was cleared by O'Connor Power's petulance and lack of judgement. On learning that Parnell had been invited to address the Westport meeting, O'Connor Power refused to attend and, in so doing, allowed his rival to reap the political benefit of all the groundwork he had done on the agrarian issue.

Parnell, to his credit, recognised that the land issue was the key to the national question, and that if he could successfully link the Home Rule movement to a popular demand like land reform, then it could catch fire. It was precisely this belief – that a fundamental link existed between the land and national questions – which lay behind the agreement on the 'New Departure'. The driving force behind the New Departure was John Devoy, the leading figure in the American Fenian movement. Devoy had been jailed for Fenian activities in 1866 and released in 1871 on condition of exile. Soon after his arrival in America Devoy joined Clan na Gael, which had been formed in 1867 in an attempt to heal the divisions in the American Fenian movement. Through his resourcefulness and determination Devoy quickly rose to the leadership of Clan na Gael, and, by the late 1870s, the Clan was the dominant force in Fenianism. Parnell's participation in the obstruction strategy and his general air of defiance had brought him to Devoy's attention, and Clan na Gael made contact with him in 1877. In the following year Devoy tried to secure Parnell's backing for a new departure style project but, at that point, the Meath MP was not ready to adopt such a risky strategy. By June 1879, however, the rapid emergence of the land issue in Mayo had altered the balance in favour of participation. Joining Devoy for the crucial meeting on 1 June 1879 were Parnell and Davitt, who listened to Devoy's proposals outlining the new strategy. It was based on the understanding that the Home Rule movement would not interfere with possible Fenian rebellion plans and, in return, Clan na Gael would provide political and financial support for Parnell as he led the campaign for Irish self-government and sought to turn the Home Rule party into a more disciplined political machine. Underpinning the New Departure was a commitment to vigorous agitation on the land issue, with peasant proprietorship as the stated objective. To some extent

O'Connor Power and his associates in Mayo had already prepared the ground for this change in direction, and Devoy was simply recognising the reality of the situation.

The New Departure symbolised the alliance between the Home Rule movement, radical agrarianism and Fenianism, and it produced a new mass movement in Irish politics, advancing the cause of nationalism under Parnell's expert leadership. While the compact was very much Devoy's agenda, it was Parnell who gained most from the New Departure. Frustrated by the inactivity of the IRB Supreme Council, whose members were unwilling to allow their separatist philosophy to be contaminated with agrarian issues, Devoy was convinced that Fenians had to participate in the agrarian movement if they were to prevent the land question extinguishing the Fenian flame altogether. At the same time, the Clan na Gael leader believed that the Westminster government would fail to solve the land question, and this would allow the Fenian movement to harness the mass support of mobilised tenant farmers in a new drive for an independent Ireland.

Although he gave the impression that he was in agreement with Devoy's analysis, Parnell's mind was working in a different direction. He sensed that the British government would move on the land question, if sufficient pressure was applied, and this success would fuel support for the political objective of Home Rule. These different interpretations added to the confusion on the outcome of the New Departure. Devoy was convinced that he had Parnell's backing for his separatist programme when, in reality, Parnell had only offered vague assurances of support for Devoy's aim of full independence. In truth, it was more likely that Parnell's participation in the New Departure was motivated by a desire to thwart Devoy's ambition, as he sought, in the short term, to involve all shades of nationalism in the agrarian struggle and then, in the longer term, transfer this energy to the political struggle for Home

Rule. Clearly Parnell wanted the support of militant nationalists but he was, at best, ambiguous in any commitments he may have made and gave little in return. Dabbling with Fenian and agrarian radicals may have appeared a risky strategy for Parnell to follow, but it was only by his participation in the New Departure that he was able to restrain militants such as Davitt.

In the summer of 1879, therefore, Parnell's immediate concern was to prevent agrarian agitation spinning out of control. Davitt had launched the Land League of Mayo in August 1879 at a meeting in Castlebar which Parnell did not attend. The new Mayo organisation, which had very solid roots, boasted a radical programme based on the rallying cry of "the land for the people". By October Davitt had made the necessary arrangements to develop a national movement, and it was really only at this point that the still cautious Parnell committed himself fully to the land agitation by accepting Davitt's invitation to become President of the Irish National Land League. Significantly, Parnell had used his influence to tone down the new movement's programme. While it continued to adhere to the idea of peasant proprietorship, the real focus was on the short-term objectives of halting evictions and reducing rents. Spreading quickly from its Mayo stronghold, the Land League established a network of branches all over the country, though it enjoyed less support in the predominantly Protestant counties in Ulster, and coordinated the campaign against landlordism. In challenging the landlords, the League mobilised the entire agricultural community and drew it inexorably towards nationalism. The League was a truly popular movement, driven from the bottom up, and outside clerical control. Local grievances were articulated and national solutions offered. The legitimacy of landlordism was questioned, and the dependence of the foreign landlord on a foreign government was repeatedly highlighted. The tactics employed by the League were brilliant and varied. It borrowed heavily from the secret society tradition and, though Parnell frequently urged his followers to use exclusively peaceful methods, violence became an effective tool. Indeed, the launch of the League in October 1879 was followed by an upsurge in the number of agrarian outrages, and the level of violence was sufficient for the period 1879–82 to become known as the 'Land War'. There had, of course, been instances of agrarian crime in the months before the establishment of the League, but the figure escalated sharply in 1880, as shootings, arson and cattle-maiming became commonplace.

There were approximately 2,500 reported agrarian outrages during 1880, and this figure almost doubled in the following year. While large areas of the country experienced agrarian violence to some degree, it was most prevalent in the western counties of Mayo, Galway and Kerry, where anxious smallholders continued to struggle with dire economic circumstances into 1880. With tenants falling behind in rent payments, the rate of eviction increased in the west, and this gave further impetus to the Land League. Within two years of its formation, the League had 200,000 members. Leadership at local level often fell to a prosperous grazier, or a shopkeeper, publican or merchant from a local town, the economic prosperity of which was totally dependent on its immediate agricultural hinterland. In this way a remarkable unity emerged between town and country as well as between the various social strata in Irish society. Fighting under "the land for the people" banner, the general aim was to transfer ownership of the land from the small group of existing landlords to a much larger number of Irish tenant farmers. Both the method and the precise outcome of such a redistribution were never clearly defined, and this allowed, in the short term at least, the establishment of a remarkable coalition of agrarian interests which saw graziers and landless labourers, previously bitter enemies, fighting together in the struggle against landlordism. Ultimately, of course, such a coalition could not be sustained. The immediate priority for the graziers was a reduction in rent, but the obvious land hunger among the landless and smallholders, particularly in the west, was certain to increase the demand for the break-up of the large grazing ranches. Yet during the brief period that the coalition held together, the Land League, by directing its fire at the institution of landlordism which became synonymous with British rule, politicised rural Catholic Ireland more effectively than any previous movement. This success was due to the raising of self-reliance among the tenant farmers and to the League's ability to give economic factors a political dimension. While it instilled the belief in the Irish farmer's mind that he had the right to own his land, the League was also regarded as a demonstration of resistance to British rule in Ireland.

The main weapons of the League were propaganda and intimidation, not violence. Local Catholic clergy were usually sympathetic to the Land League branches which were organised on a parish basis, and the provincial press was solidly behind the new movement. Undoubtedly, increased literacy rates played their part in spreading the League's message. While the Land League was an open and legal organisation, frequently stressing the use of non-violent methods and a commitment to moral force, its leaders, both at local and national level, understood the value of violence. Beginning in the west, violence became widespread, but was never endemic. It did, of course, attract a huge amount of publicity but, measured against the level of agrarian protest, the violence was restrained. Moreover, agrarian crime was very much local in character, a response to local economic factors. In 1878 the rate of evictions doubled from the previous year, and this figure continued to rise before reaching a peak in the spring of 1882. Not surprisingly, there was a close correlation between evictions and local agitation. Over the course of the Land War 67 murders were committed. Only a minority of this figure were landlords, land agents or others acting in the landed interest. Of the others, it seems that many of the killings were the result of local disputes in which the guilty parties used the cover of agrarian unrest to settle old scores. In truth, violence was effective during the Land War because it was sufficient to ensure that intimidation, the League's key weapon, had the desired outcome. This was widely successful in the application of the boycott, a campaign of social ostracism mounted against selected individuals and backed by the threat of violence. Indeed, it was this combination of moral and physical force that made the League's prosecution of the Land War so effective. Though motivated by local economic concerns, violence became political in character. It was condoned not just by militant agrarians such as Davitt, but by Parnell and his followers in the Home Rule party, who viewed it as tactical. In this way the Land War contributed to the culture of violence and rejection of authority which was to be a feature of rural society for successive generations of nationalists. Above all, however, the land agitation witnessed widespread participation at grass roots level, and tactics such as the boycott were all the more effective because they were based on unity and collective action.

In this way the Land League developed as a mass movement able to channel the energy and enthusiasm released by the agrarian agitation into an effective strategy. Its meetings, usually held on Sundays, drew large crowds and, while a carnival atmosphere usually existed, those who attended were conscious of the fact that they were engaged in the defiance of authority. In essence, the League was about confrontation, and the target was British state power, not just the local landlord. Much of its success was due to its ability to mobilise the entire rural population on the land issue. There was, of course, some involvement by Fenians who were keen to exploit popular grievances in the hope that this would ultimately produce more widespread support for their revolutionary designs. The fact that violence was restrained also encouraged the participation of the Catholic Church, and this was particularly true of the lower clergy. Indeed, the open involvement of the Fenian element at both local and national level acted as a spur to the Church, which was anxious to provide a counterbalance to possible Fenian extremism. More important than the Fenian contribution, however, was the involvement in the land issue of Home Rule politicians eager to make political capital out of agrarian discontent. These men engaged with the masses in a direct way and, in the process, Irish nationalism, previously the complex preserve of the educated middle classes, became open and relevant for the great mass of people in the country. It was the timely appearance of this inspirational and dynamic political leadership that transformed the impressive mobilisation of rural Ireland into the kernel of a powerful nationalist movement. With all these groups on board, the Land League allowed Catholic Ireland to present a much more sharply defined version of nationality than anything that had been possible in the O'Connell era. At the same time, land and nationalism became inextricably bound together in the last quarter of the nineteenth century.

If the Land League was to fight evictions and support evicted tenants, it needed money. Consequently, in December 1879, Parnell travelled to America on a fund-raising mission, collecting a sum of £30,000 within two months. This provided the League with a solid financial footing and enabled it to appoint full time organisers to coordinate the agitation. News of an impending general election in April 1880 brought Parnell back to Ireland, and he intended to use the campaign to strengthen his grip on the Home Rule party. His chief rival was William Shaw who had acted as party chairman following Butt's death and, by May 1880, Parnell had defeated the moderate Shaw in a leadership election by 23 votes to 18. The bedrock of Parnell's support was in Connacht, a testament to the Land League's strength in the west, and the majority of new MPs were firmly behind Parnell's leadership. Among the new influx was John Dillon, the son of the Young Irelander John Blake Dillon. Dillon, who had accompanied Parnell on his American tour, was one of a new breed of Home Rule politicians. A militant agrarian and very able organiser who established a network of contacts all over Ireland, Dillon and his young radical colleagues provided the necessary dynamic leadership on the ground which contributed to the League's spectacular growth. The accompanying agitation and the defiance of the Land League demanded a response from the government. A carrot-and-stick policy, combining conciliation and coercion, was the favoured option of Gladstone's Liberal government. Coercive legislation came into force in the early part of 1881 and this led to the arrest of a number of prominent land agitators. Parnell and his followers provided fierce opposition to the Coercion Bill, and they were ejected from the House of Commons when they caused uproar in protesting against Davitt's arrest. Reports of the chaotic scenes at Westminster drew appreciation among Parnell's supporters in Ireland and the experience helped to forge the Home Rule party into a more cohesive force in Parliament. Yet Parnell now faced a dilemma. He had a choice to make between withdrawing to Ireland and staking all on further agitation or working the constitutional process and building up support in Parliament. To the dismay of the militant agrarians, he chose the constitutional path.

The government's coercion tactics failed to stem the unrest in Ireland, but Gladstone unveiled the conciliation element in his Irish policy when he introduced a new Land Bill in 1881. Parnell's constitutional approach appeared to have paid rapid dividends. Gladstone's bill became law in August and it granted the three Fs – fair rent, free sale and fixity of tenure. This was a major piece of legislation because it established the basis for a new relationship between landlord and tenant, ultimately easing the transition towards peasant ownership. Of course, the balance still lay with the landlords, but it seemed to them that Parnell and the Land League had forced intolerable concessions on a weak government. For the more radical agrarians, however, the 1881 Land Act was woefully inadequate, and, in his attempt to hold his agrarian coalition together, Parnell expressed his dissatisfaction with the legislation. At the same time, Parnell recognised the significance of the concessions granted by the government and he persuaded the Land League to "test the act", arguing that this was the best way to expose its limitations. Although his privately held views were much more moderate, Parnell was anxious to maintain the League's momentum and he deliberately chose violent language to denounce the Land Act. Fortunately for his immediate political future, the government reacted to his intemperate outbursts by arresting him in October 1881, thereby shielding him from the consequences of a Land League split. With Parnell and many of the other leaders in Kilmainham jail, a new burst of agrarian unrest was unleashed. From his prison cell Parnell, bowing to pressure from his colleagues, issued a 'No Rent' manifesto on 18 October, urging the tenants to withhold rent payments. As a result, the Land League was suppressed and, as Parnell had predicted, the manifesto proved to be a flop. In effect, the Land Act, in providing assistance to the more prosperous tenant farmers, opened up a serious division among the rural population, which the League had been struggling to contain.

Naturally, Parnell's imprisonment had inflamed the situation in rural Ireland, particularly in Connacht, but the main reason for the steep rise in violence was the reaction of the poorer tenant farmers who fell outside the scope of Gladstone's Land Act. Between October 1880 and April 1882 almost 3,500 instances of agrarian crime were reported, as law and order completely broke down over many areas in the west of the country. On his arrest Parnell had predicted that 'Captain Moonlight' would take his place, but he quickly became alarmed at the scale of the violence and was anxious to see it halted. So was Gladstone, and this prompted him to broker a deal with Parnell. The result of this unofficial agreement was the 'Kilmainham Treaty'. Parnell was released on 2 May 1882, giving vague assurances about using his influence to calm the situation in the Irish countryside and offering only general support for the Liberal government's progressive measures. In return, the government promised to drop coercion and make arrangements to have rent arrears wiped out. Soon, an Arrears Act provided £800,000 worth of relief for approximately 130,000 tenants who had fallen behind with their rents. Before this, however, the brutal murder in Dublin's Phoenix Park of the new Chief Secretary, Lord Frederick Cavendish, and his Under-Secretary, TH Burke, only four days after Parnell's release from Kilmainham, shocked opinion in Britain and Ireland. The Invincibles, a secret group of violent nationalists who had broken away from the Fenian movement, had carried out the attack. Parnell was horrified by the murders and even considered withdrawing from politics. A new coercion measure followed and all shades of nationalism were attacked in the English press. In Ireland itself widespread revulsion was a common reaction to the Phoenix Park atrocity, and Parnell was more determined than ever to bring all agitation to an end and focus nationalist energy on his political agenda. This was facilitated by the impact of the Arrears Act, which had done much to calm the situation in the agrarian heartlands, and by the economic upswing as agricultural prices gradually recovered.

The Land League had served its purpose and was not revived. In its place Parnell established the Irish National League in October 1882, but its aims were clearly more political in character with emphasis being laid on the advancement of the Home Rule cause. Although it was a highly centralised organisation which gave less scope to grass roots activists, it continued and developed the work done by the Land League in raising political consciousness across nationalist Ireland. It was also very much under Parnell's control, and a measure of his personal popularity and recognised authority can be gauged from the £37,000 raised by the National League and handed over to the Irish leader. This was welcomed by a heavily indebted Parnell, and the collection was reminiscent of the gratitude once shown to O'Connell for his contribution to Irish nationalism. Again, the National League was able to swallow the Land League's structures at local level and it soon had branches all over Ireland. From 1883 to 1885 the land question became subordinated to the national question as local grievances were increasingly linked to the demand for self-government. Moreover, the principle of Home Rule, hitherto a rather vague concept in rural Ireland, became more attractive as the belief took hold that only an Irish parliament could fully understand Irish problems. While Parnell kept a firm grip on the reins of power, he allowed his able young lieutenants, who had demonstrated their leadership abilities during the Land War, a good measure of freedom and they worked energetically to establish a new political momentum at local level. At the same time, the social composition of the Home Rule party was changing. Farmers and shopkeepers were becoming more prominent, and this trend was highlighted by the 1885 general election in which the number of petty bourgeois representatives rose sharply. There was also a significant increase in the number of Catholic Home Rulers. The Church had overcome its early misgivings about endorsing a Protestant leader and threw its considerable weight behind the campaign for Home Rule which, it accepted, was the best way to advance its own claims and satisfy the needs of its flock. The Home Rule party, or Irish Parliamentary Party (IPP) as it was often known, developed rapidly into a highly disciplined and effective political instrument. Its MPs were paid out of party funds and the 'parliamentary pledge', introduced in 1884, committed all Home Rule MPs to vote together on all occasions when the majority decided that the party should act in unison. Two further developments strengthened Parnell's party. The 1884 Reform Act more than trebled the number of Irish men eligible to vote, from 220,000 to over 700,000. Most of the new voters were small tenant farmers, thereby solidifying the IPP's social base. This was augmented by the Redistribution Act of 1885 which reduced the representation of the boroughs.

A demonstration of the power which a disciplined Home Rule party could bring to bear at Westminster came in June 1885, when the IPP joined with the Conservatives to turn the Liberal government out of office. Parnell had been unhappy at Gladstone's reluctance to embrace Home Rule, and his action had demonstrated that the IPP could make or break governments at Westminster if the political arithmetic allowed. Although the minority Conservative administration quickly introduced an imaginative land purchase measure, which set a pattern for future land reform, the Prime Minster, Lord Salisbury, was not prepared to risk major political changes which, he was certain, would throw his own party into crisis. Indeed, the failure of the two great Westminster parties to agree on a bipartisan approach to Ireland created further opportunities for Parnell who had clearly been successful in forcing the Irish question to the top of the political agenda in London. In the general election of 1885 the IPP with its 86 seats held the balance of power, as the Conservatives won 249 seats to the Liberals' 335 seats. Still frustrated by the Liberals' rejection of his Home Rule demand, Parnell had used his influence during the election campaign to persuade Irish voters in Britain to support Conservative candidates. Undoubtedly, this cost the Liberals a number of seats and strengthened Parnell's hand in the new Parliament. In view of the Conservative party's subsequent passionate defence of the Union, Parnell's actions may appear self-defeating, but the political reality in 1885 was that either of the two great Westminster parties could have taken up the Home Rule cause in order to wrong-foot their opponents. The 1885 general election also proved to be a defining moment in Irish politics, sketching, as it did, a new political landscape which would remain largely unaltered until 1918. Nationalism was now the dominant force in Ireland. The Liberal party had been decimated and the Conservatives had retreated into their Ulster strongholds.

Both parties at Westminster recognised that a response to this development could not be avoided. Parnell had made the IPP a force at Westminster and Home Rule was now a live issue. He had squeezed land reforms from both main parties, but this had merely whetted his supporters' desire for further concessions. Parnellism reflected this growing Irish self-confidence. It had been built on solid agrarian foundations as the land issue had politicised the masses. Although he himself was a good landlord with a genuine sympathy for the peasantry, Parnell knew how to exploit landlord–tenant conflict in order to advance his own political agenda. The land agitation was simply a means to an end, and it allowed him to win control of the political movement as he concentrated on parliamentary activity and the struggle for Home Rule. While nationalism was clearly rooted in the Irish soil and was the political creed of the dominant tenant farming class, the main theatre of activity, as far as Parnell was concerned, was Westminster. Unquestionably, he was a unifying force, carrying with him moderate nationalists, radical agrarians and constitutional Fenians. This allowed him to control his extremist followers and benefit from their support. Moreover, his National League, like the earlier Land League, was also successful in pulling together the various elements in Irish society. This coalition of rural and urban, prosperous farmer and landless labourer, gave Parnellism its mass following. This was consolidated by the leader's charisma and the deference shown by his key followers. But, as Paul Bew has pointed out, Parnell had another project. His aim was to find a compromise which would end the conflict between landlord and tenant. If accomplished, this would allow a reformed landlord class to join with him in the struggle for Home Rule and, thereby, enhance its prospects of success. Parnell's view of his fellow landlords was obviously naive, but he was astute enough to realise that the tenant farmers' ultimate aim was to own their holdings. More radical alternatives such as Davitt's plans for 'Land Nationalisation' were largely ignored and this made the movement more conservative and in tune with Parnell and, therefore, easier to control. Parnell also recognised that his political movement would be Catholic, and he had been careful to ensure that his speeches did not alienate the Catholic Church. By isolating Davitt and the radicals, Parnell also made it easier for the Church to play a full part in Home Rule politics.

In this way the parallels between O'Connellism and Parnellism were strengthened though, of course, essential differences remained. As was the case with O'Connell and repeal, Parnell never offered a precise definition of Home Rule, nor did he commit himself to give a clear undertaking that Home Rule should be regarded as a final constitutional settlement. This left Home Rule as a catch-all ideology which could hold the support of all shades of nationalist opinion. Parnellism received a further boost with the bizarre events of December 1885, when news was leaked that Gladstone was now in favour of Home Rule. Clearly, Parnellism had also influenced the great Liberal leader, though questions remain both about Gladstone's motives and the speed of his conversion. Back in government, Gladstone began preparations for the Home Rule Bill which was introduced in April 1886. Previously, the essential core of Parnellism had been the pragmatism of a highly disciplined IPP which acted independently of the great English parties in order to force concessions from both of them. By temperament, it seems that Parnell would have preferred to work with the Conservative party, but Gladstone's dramatic conversion nudged him into an alliance with the Liberals. While this may have been the only practical course open to the Irish leader, it rendered Parnellism less effective. On the surface, Home Rule meant simply giving a new Irish parliament control over domestic affairs, but this masks the complex nature of the financial and constitutional arrangements deemed necessary for the smooth working of this devolution experiment. For both Gladstone and Parnell, moreover, Home Rule had to be accompanied by the introduction of a comprehensive land purchase scheme which would reconcile the landlord class and allow its members to assume a prominent role in any new devolved parliament.

The combined support of IPP and Liberal MPs should have guaranteed the Home Rule Bill's passage in the House of Commons, but, in the event, the measure was defeated by 343 votes to 313. The Liberal party had split on the issue, with 93 Liberal MPs voting against Home Rule. Gladstone had been deserted by the party's old Whig element which shared Conservative fears that Home Rule would cause long-term damage to the Empire. More significantly, a large group of radical Liberals led by Joseph Chamberlain was fiercely opposed to Gladstone's new Irish strategy. Chamberlain was adamant that Home Rule would destroy the Union, warning that it would never satisfy Irish nationalists who, he claimed, would continue to demand incremental progress towards complete separation. Indeed, some of Parnell's speeches, including his celebrated Cork speech in January 1885, had warned that "no man has the right to fix the boundary to the march of a nation", suggesting that Home Rule would be viewed as a first instalment rather than a final settlement. Of course, Parnell's own views were more moderate than his public statements. Such rhetoric had the two-fold purpose of laying down a marker for future negotiations and maintaining unity among the various factions supporting Parnell. But the influential Chamberlain had raised another objection to Home Rule. He argued that public opinion in Britain would not accept the abandonment of fellow Anglo-Saxon Protestants living in Ulster, but both Gladstone and Parnell played down the threat that Ulster posed to Home Rule. Although the details of the Home Rule Bill of 1886 seem fairly innocuous, as the powers granted to the new Irish parliament were strictly limited, the passions aroused by the proposals were unprecedented. In the end, the issue was settled by the defection of so many Liberals, but the arguments would be repeated over the next 30 years.

Two days after the Home Rule Bill's defeat Parliament was dissolved, but Gladstone's appeal to the electorate on the issue was firmly rejected. In the general election of July 1886 the Conservatives won a landslide victory as the Liberals were reduced to only 191 seats. The IPP repeated its success of the previous year but, with the new Conservative government expressing outright opposition to Irish self-government, Parnell had little room to manoeuvre. He had come close to bringing off a spectacular triumph, but the prospects for the future success of Home Rule now clearly depended on the future prospects of Gladstone's Liberal party. For Parnell, the old strategy of independent action at Westminster was no longer an option. Closer cooperation with the Liberals had to be developed, and Parnell recognised that any renewal of agrarian agitation might place an intolerable strain on the Liberal alliance. Yet most indicators pointed to a renewal of the Land War in the autumn of 1886. A downturn in agricultural prices, which began in 1885 and continued into 1886, brought more hardship to the tenant farmers. Moreover, the political vacuum created by the defeat of the Home Rule Bill encouraged Parnell's more militant followers to return to land agitation. These men regarded agrarian agitation as an assertion of their nationalist rights and were convinced that a combination of political action and agrarian agitation was the best way to advance the nationalist cause.

The two most prominent radical agrarians, John Dillon and William O'Brien, were responsible for directing the Plan of Campaign, the title given to the new phase of the Land War which was launched in October 1886. The essence of the Plan was to target individual estates and offer these landlords a reduced rent. If this was refused, the money was paid into an estate fund which was used to compensate individual tenants who faced eviction as a consequence of their actions. The operation of the Plan was confined to approximately 200 estates, most of which had been selected because the landlord was known to be in financial difficulty and was, therefore, more susceptible to pressure. Again, most of the activity took place in the south and west where tenant distress was most acute. Physical violence, intimidation and the boycott also resurfaced, but the Plan never enjoyed the success achieved by the Land League and suffered from lack of funds. By the end of 1890 the agitation had petered out in the face of resolute action taken by Salisbury's Conservative government, which developed a tough security policy to combat the agitation. While this served the government's immediate purpose and, incidentally, paved the way for an imaginative series of Conservative reforms in Ireland, participation in the conflict had, once again, strengthened the unity of purpose within nationalist ranks. Therefore, the land question retained the ability to transform Irish nationalism into a united and cohesive force.

Parnell was not involved in the new wave of agitation associated with the Plan. Indeed, as early as December 1886, he had sought to restrain Dillon and O'Brien and curb the level of agitation. Whereas Parnell's radical lieutenants believed that a renewal of the land agitation was necessary to maintain nationalist momentum, their leader was concerned about the problems that widespread agitation would create for the Liberal alliance. He was adamant that the land issue had served its purpose, and he played no part in the implementation of the Plan. In the late 1880s Parnell's primary focus was on the political aim of Home Rule, and he became much more concerned with English, rather than Irish, public opinion. But Parnell had more personal reasons for his refusal to become embroiled in the Irish land question at this point. In 1880 he had begun a liaison with Katherine O'Shea, the wife of one of his parliamentary colleagues and, by 1886, the couple were living together in Eltham, south-east London. Spending most of his time with Mrs O'Shea, Parnell, who was often in ill-health, neglected his role as IPP leader at Westminster and rarely crossed to Ireland, leaving others to promote the nationalist cause at home. Parnell had always been cold and aloof with his Irish colleagues, but his frequent absences now dented his authority.

This relationship with Mrs O'Shea was an open secret. Many of Parnell's political associates were aware of the relationship and Katherine's estranged husband, Captain William O'Shea, not only connived at the affair but sought to exploit it for his own political advancement. Indeed, Parnell had pulled more than a few strings to have Captain O'Shea adopted as the IPP candidate in the Galway City by-election in February 1886. Opposition to O'Shea's selection was led by the able Tim Healy, a leading Home Rule MP who never forgave Parnell for his roughshod tactics in the selection procedure. O'Shea had not taken the parliamentary pledge and he actually refused to support the Home Rule Bill only four months after his election. Following this dramatic twist, O'Shea resigned his seat knowing that he could expect no further political favours from Parnell. Yet the Irish leader also knew that it was only the prospect of a sizeable bequest from Katherine's ageing aunt that prevented O'Shea from initiating divorce proceedings. This situation was unlikely to continue, and Parnell must have been aware of the threat which a messy divorce case might pose to his political future.

Still, all this lay ahead. Before the divorce case shocked Victorian Britain, Parnell was involved in another legal tangle which enhanced his reputation on the mainland. In 1887 *The Times* ran a series of articles under the heading "Parnellism and Crime", alleging that Parnell and his party had been involved in criminal acts. The articles were based on letters, supposedly written by Parnell, the most damaging of which expressed the Irish leader's regret in having to condemn the Phoenix Park murders. The Conservative government hoped to expose Parnell's murky past by establishing a special commission to investigate the charges, but the plan backfired when, in February 1889, the letters were found to be forgeries.

This dramatic news raised Parnell's stature to new heights, particularly in England, but, in December 1889, six months after the death of Katherine's rich aunt, an angry O'Shea, who had been passed over in the will, filed a petition for divorce, citing Parnell as co-respondent. Before the case came to court in November 1890 Parnell had assured his associates that his career would not suffer, but the details that emerged in court cast Parnell in a squalid light. Despite the revelations, the IPP nervously gave him their unanimous backing but, within a week, the situation had been reversed once it became known that the Liberal party, which contained a powerful nonconformist wing, would not, in spite of Gladstone's efforts, continue in alliance with the IPP while Parnell remained as leader. On 6 December 1890 the Home Rule MPs, meeting in the House of Commons, faced the agonising dilemma of choosing between Home Rule and Parnell. Amid bitter acrimony they chose Home Rule, and Parnell was deposed a leader. Immediately, the party split into two unequal factions, with the minority remaining loyal to Parnell. If the "Chief" was unnerved by this sequence of events, he did not show it. Parnell gave notice that he would battle for his reinstatement and decided to take the fight to Ireland, declaring that he owed his position as leader to the people of Ireland, not to his fellow Irish MPs. The episode had also demonstrated that Parnell's political strategy after 1886 had weakened his authority in both the party and the country, while his autocratic style of leadership had created a number of bitter personal enemies who now sought revenge.

Parnell was given a rapturous welcome on his return to Dublin, but it soon emerged that he would face insurmountable opposition in Ireland. The Catholic Church, which had maintained a low profile during the divorce proceedings, finally came off the fence as the hierarchy switched sides and denounced the former leader. Of course, a good part of Parnell's legacy was based on his heroic struggle against impossible odds in the final nine months of his life. During this period Parnell demonstrated that his political skills had not been diminished by his self-imposed exile, and his performance was, at times, reminiscent of the heady days of 1879–81, when he had pushed constitutionalism to its limits. However, his failure to rally the people was confirmed by crushing defeats for Parnell's candidates in three crucial by-elections when the influence of the Church proved decisive. During these campaigns Parnell seized every opportunity to attack his opponents, but it was clear that he was becoming increasingly desperate. He appealed directly to 'the hillside men', as he sought electoral support from Fenian sympathisers who had backed him in his early career. These violent speeches were an indication of Parnell's profound sense of despair rather than a change of political direction. Parnell never abandoned constitutional politics and he retained sufficient vision to warn of the dangers inherent in narrow sectarian nationalism, arguing that the Catholic majority in Ireland needed to adopt a more conciliatory, accommodating attitude towards their fellow Irishmen. Yet such was the bitter feeling aroused by the leadership struggle that this kind of perceptive analysis was lost among the personal invective.

The exertions of Parnell's Irish campaign had taken its toll on his health and he died in October 1891 following a short illness. His funeral in Dublin drew a crowd estimated at 200,000, as a shocked Ireland had to come to terms with his tragic and premature death. A testament to Parnell's great ability to unite all shades of nationalism was the way in which he came to be regarded as an inspiration to both constitutional and revolutionary nationalists.

The leadership feud had done serious damage to constitutional nationalism, and the split continued with even greater bitterness after Parnell's death. In the general election of July 1892 the anti-Parnellites, as they had become known, won 71 seats, while the Parnellite group under John Redmond won only nine seats. However, this rout of the Parnellites was not as complete as these figures suggest. Outside Ulster, Parnellite candidates had secured one-third of the votes cast and they had polled particularly well in urban areas. Redmond blamed clerical influence for the Parnellites' poor showing in rural constituencies, but the key reason for the success of the anti-Parnellites was the electors' belief in the argument that only the maintenance of the Liberal alliance could deliver Home Rule. Redmond's call for a return to independent opposition at Westminster was rejected, and the anti-Parnellites appeared to be vindicated when a second Home Rule Bill was introduced in February 1893. The general election of the previous year had returned Gladstone and the Liberals to government and, once again, the Irish party held the balance of power. Although his party remained nervous on the Home Rule issue, Gladstone's personal commitment was beyond question. Furthermore, at the end of a very long political career, the great Liberal leader was determined to bring peace to Ireland and regarded Home Rule as a moral necessity. While he was, by this stage, more aware of Ulster opposition to any Home Rule scheme, he firmly rejected all demands for special treatment and the main features of the 1886 Bill were retained. Every clause of the second Home Rule Bill was bitterly contested as the discussion process dragged on for 82 days, but Gladstone's nerve held and the measure was passed by a majority of 34 in the House of Commons. Irish nationalists were jubilant, but Gladstone had calculated that he needed a majority of 100 in order to force the Lords' hand on the issue. Even this was wishful thinking and, in September 1893, the House of Lords overwhelmingly rejected the second Home Rule Bill. Gladstone was ready to continue the struggle, but his party shared neither his vision nor his enthusiasm. In 1894 he retired from politics and the Liberal party put Home Rule on the back burner.

The IPP split had not helped Gladstone's efforts to sell Home Rule to his Liberal backbenchers. Indeed, Redmond, the Parnellite leader, had openly criticised certain aspects of the 1893 Bill, when many assumed that the measure would highlight the need for an end to division within nationalism. The split continued through the general election of July 1895 in which the anti-Parnellites won 70 seats, leaving Redmond's group with only 11 seats. The 1895 contest also revealed the increased political apathy in Ireland following the damage done by the Parnell split. Only 42 of the seats were contested, a figure which was down by 50 per cent on the 1892 level. The fact that Home Rule was off the agenda at Westminster naturally dampened enthusiasm, but there was also a sense of disgust among grass roots nationalists who had been demoralised and embarrassed by the spectacle of the split and the subsequent petty squabbling among the various factions struggling for control. Constitutional nationalism had been discredited. While Redmond repeatedly charged his opponents with betrayal, there was, if anything, even greater division among the anti-Parnellite majority. On his removal as chairman of the Irish party in December 1890, Parnell had been replaced by Justin McCarthy. Though he was popular and highly regarded by many of his parliamentary colleagues, McCarthy had neither the authority nor the force of personality to maintain unity among the anti-Parnellite group of MPs. The two heavyweights in the movement were John Dillon and Tim Healy and, from the early days of the Home Rule movement, they had been highly suspicious of each other. In addition to their bitter personal rivalry, however, there were significant ideological differences between the two.

Healy was from the clericalist right wing of the party. He wanted more power devolved to constituency level, particularly in relation to the selection of candidates, where local priests would be in a position to exercise more influence. Moreover, Healy did not subscribe to the argument that the Liberal alliance should form the basis of IPP strategy. This put him at odds with Dillon. Though a devout Catholic, Dillon was consistent in his opposition to clerical participation in politics. Furthermore, he was determined to retain the powerful central authority that had been established by Parnell. This put Dillon and Healy on a collision course. Gladstone's retirement from politics in 1894 ensured that the Liberal party's enthusiasm for Home Rule would never reach its previous level, but Dillon clung to the belief that all the Irish party's efforts should be concentrated on securing Home Rule and that the only way to achieve this was by fostering the Liberal alliance.

Even the Conservative victory in the 1895 general election did not shake Dillon's confidence. By this stage the rivalry between the Dillonite and Healyite factions had burst into the open as each side sought to have their supporters nominated for safe IPP seats. In the general election Dillon enjoyed a narrow advantage, and he was determined to press this home in the immediate post-election period. Matters came to a head, when a by-election was held in South Kerry in September

1895. Healy had moved quickly to persuade local clergy in the constituency to endorse the candidature of one of his closest supporters, but Dillon insisted that an 'official party' candidate should contest the seat. After an extremely bitter campaign Dillon's nominee was declared the victor. In February 1896 Dillon replaced McCarthy as party chairman, and he would use his new role to expel Healy and his supporters, whom he accused of disloyalty and insubordination, from positions of influence within the party's organisation. Although this had been achieved by the end of 1896, Healy continued to enjoy a measure of support within nationalist circles. In January 1897, with considerable clerical support, Healy launched the People's Rights Association as a rival to the National Federation, the Irish party's organisation, but his efforts to create a conservative Catholic party and, simultaneously, undermine Dillon met with failure.

Dillon had won the power struggle, but the faction fighting of the 1890s had discredited constitutional nationalism. The constant sniping between the Redmondites, the Healyites and the Dillonites in the mid-1890s provided a sharp contrast to the unity and cohesion established by Parnell during the early 1880s. Moreover, the land issue was no longer the dynamic economic factor that had energised Irish nationalism. Successive Conservative governments, beginning in 1885, had sought to remove the land question from the nationalist equation. In a sense, therefore, Lord Salisbury's Conservative government was acknowledging that the land question and the national question were inseparable. Based on the principle of land purchase, the Treasury provided funds to compensate landlords and allow tenants to purchase their holdings. Dillon was suspicious of Conservative intentions, believing that land purchase might, as the Conservatives themselves hoped, dilute Irish nationalism and, thereby, reduce the demand for Home Rule. Initially, these government subsidies were given a lukewarm reception by Irish tenants, who considered the financial terms imposed by the state to be unattractive. The Conservative government was moving in the right direction, but it would take the generous terms offered by the 1903 Wyndham Act to achieve the overhaul of land tenure which, ultimately, the state, the landlords and the tenants desired.

Before this, however, the land question, once again, demonstrated its capacity to mobilise the tenant farming class. A new wave of agrarian agitation broke out in Connacht in 1896, as the familiar pattern of poor harvests and economic hardship returned. The key figure in channelling the new agrarian protest movement was William O'Brien, who had established his credentials as an agrarian campaigner during the days of the Land League and the Plan of Campaign. O'Brien had been a close associate of Dillon's, but he had retired as an MP in 1895, dismayed by the Irish party's failure to resolve its differences. Settling in County Mayo, O'Brien was immediately struck by the suffering of the Connacht smallholders, and then witnessed, at first hand, the impact of the failure of the potato crop in 1896 and 1897 and the fear of a new famine. Initially, O'Brien assumed that it would take a reunited Irish party under Dillon's leadership to direct the agitation but, when his efforts to draw the warring factions together were frustrated, O'Brien turned away from his former parliamentary colleagues and looked to grass roots activists in Connacht.

On 23 January 1898, at a public gathering in Westport, O'Brien launched the United Irish League (UIL). Through the new movement O'Brien sought to channel the agitation which, naturally, saw a return to the successful tactics used by the Land League. Indeed, many historians take the view that the Land War can best be understood as a conflict which ran from 1879, and the birth of the Land League, to 1903, and the Wyndham Act, with the UIL dominating the final phase of the agitation. Unlike the previous campaigns, when the Protestant landlord was the target of the agitation, the UIL focused its attention on local Catholic graziers. In raising the cry of "the land for the people", O'Brien was demanding the break-up of both the estates and the grazing ranches. Significantly, the UIL also introduced the concept of compulsory purchase, which it regarded as the best way to achieve its aim of tenant ownership. Facing this new challenge of agrarian protest, the government responded in a predictable manner by turning to coercion. In the late 1890s, however, all the ingredients for successful agitation in the west were in place and, under O'Brien's brilliant, inspirational leadership, the UIL overcame government resistance. Although it never generated the popular enthusiasm of the early 1880s, O'Brien managed to mould spasmodic agrarian outrages into a coherent organisation that claimed over 50,000 members within two years of its formation.

But O'Brien also had a political motive in launching his agrarian movement, because he hoped to use the UIL to reunite the Irish party. In addition to reinvigorating Irish nationalism and maintaining pressure for reform, O'Brien believed that the land issue could provide the common ground to enable the various factions to work together. Yet, in seeking party unity, O'Brien came into conflict with his old colleague, Dillon, who feared that the new focus on agrarian activity would divert nationalist energy from the Home Rule struggle. Still, by the end of 1898, Dillon had recognised that the UIL would not go away and he sought to make the best of the situation by agreeing that the UIL should replace the National Federation as the party's organisation. In spite of his lack of enthusiasm, it was clear that grass roots activity, or pressure from below, rather than Dillon's preference for high politics, was pushing the party towards reunion. Significantly, the League made a major impact in the local government elections of 1899 following the overhaul of local government in the previous year. Although O'Brien succeeded in using the UIL to unite Dillonites, Healyites and Redmondites, his hope that a reunited party would continue to press the League's agrarian programme was not fulfilled. In his effort to reunite the party O'Brien was aided by Dillon's resignation, made in a fit of pique, from the leadership of the anti-Parnellite group. This allowed him to secure agreement between Redmond and Healy and, fearing isolation and the further loss of influence, Dillon then threw his support behind the reunion attempts.

After nearly ten years of bitter feuding the IPP was formally reunited on 30 January 1900. Dillon had taken the decisive step of outlining a programme that provided the basis for unity. He advocated a return to the old party's constitution and declared that the reunited party would pursue an independent line at Westminster, where it would concentrate on securing Home Rule but would also fight for social and economic reforms which would be of benefit to Ireland. Crucially, Dillon bowed to pressure from O'Brien and, on 6 February 1900, Redmond was declared the unanimous choice to lead the reunited party. In June the UIL was formally integrated into the party and was officially accepted as the IPP's nationalist organisation.

Although the party had been reunited under Redmond's chairmanship, it never recaptured the dynamism of the early Parnellite period. The land issue had breathed life into constitutional nationalism and transformed the IPP into a vibrant, dynamic movement, led by a charismatic personality. The party became a highly disciplined and effective political instrument, and it enjoyed a mass following in the county. This made constitutional nationalism an umbrella movement, drawing support from the various social strata in Catholic Ireland. Parnell had moved swiftly to control and contain his radical agrarian followers once this successful mobilisation had been achieved, but the split of 1890–91 brought many of these long-standing tensions to the surface.

In the last quarter of the nineteenth century the land and the national questions had become inseparable. All those involved in the agrarian movement were instinctive, if not political, nationalists. Home Rule remained their core ideological belief, based on the simple assumption that only an Irish administration could solve Irish problems. But this ignored Westminster's success in overcoming the land problem. Having established the principle of land purchase, it only remained for the government to put together a comprehensive package backed by generous funding to resolve the land question. Although agrarian agitation was revived spasmodically in the early years of the twentieth century, the 1903 Wyndham Act had achieved its purpose. It was the result of an agreement between landlord and tenant, appealing to the landlord by providing a 12 per cent bonus for the sale of an entire estate, and to the tenant by ensuring that annual repayments were lower than existing rents. This enabled the majority of tenant farmers to become owner-occupiers. Ultimately, the legislation also altered the relationship between land and nationalism, but this was not recognised by the IPP. Indeed, the land question had become so ingrained in Irish political culture that it continued to influence social and political relationships well into the twentieth century.

5

The Development of Cultural Nationalism

THE UPHEAVAL WITHIN constitutional nationalism during the 1890s encouraged the growth of other forms of nationalism. The IPP had been discredited and something of a vacuum had been created within Irish political life. It was also true that this period saw a greater focus on the corrupt nature of nationalist politics, particularly at local level where a sophisticated patronage machine often operated. Even as the UIL sought to bring an end to the internal feuding and unite the party from below, it was attacked by urban intellectuals who scoffed at the League's narrow agrarian agenda. Such people were drawn to cultural nationalism which was to develop as a significant force at the end of the nineteenth century. Previously, constitutional nationalists had given little thought to Ireland's cultural identity, but this was challenged by new thinking in Irish intellectual circles that political nationalism had to be reinforced by a strong cultural dimension if it was to meet with success. Parnell's dominance and the aura of infallibility associated with the Chief had discouraged any such deviation, but his removal and the hitherto concealed weakness of the IPP had clearly altered the situation. Moreover, European influences had suggested that the development of a cultural identity was a necessary prerequisite for the advance of political nationalism and this oversight had to be belatedly addressed.

At another level the awakening of cultural nationalism can be viewed as a reaction against the modernisation of Irish society in the second half of the nineteenth century. The upheaval caused by the myriad of social and economic changes had contributed to an identity crisis in Irish society and encouraged those affected to look backwards in search of their cultural and historical roots. Significantly, many of those drawn to cultural nationalism, usually urban intellectuals, had, up to that point, shown little interest in political nationalism. They experienced a general feeling of insecurity and they were opposed to the remorseless advance of commercialisation. This brought them into conflict with political nationalism which had, of course, benefited from economic developments such as the spread of the railways and the rapid growth of newspapers. In fact, constitutional nationalists had sought to reflect such modernisation and, in their commitment to the Liberal alliance, leading figures such as Dillon identified wholeheartedly with the progressive social policies of British Liberalism.

There was, however, another group in Irish society which was interested in political nationalism but found it a closed shop. The modernisation of Irish society had increased the numbers and importance of the educated lower middle classes, the petty bourgeoisie, who felt excluded from political life by the forces of old nationalism. This older generation, which had been blooded in the early days of the Land League, enjoyed a stranglehold on the party and its organisation at both local and national level. Frustrated by their exclusion and yet retaining political ambition, these younger petty bourgeois elements quickly became disillusioned with conventional politics and, not surprisingly, were attracted to cultural nationalism. This conflict between old and new nationalism was a reflection of a wider generational conflict which was an important feature of contemporary society, while new nationalism also provided a forum for women to engage in cultural and political life. Yet it was not only political mobility that was impeded. Rapid social and economic changes had raised expectations among the petty bourgeoisie, but the path to higher status, particularly in public employment, was often blocked by Protestants. In time, therefore, cultural nationalism developed a strong populist Catholic edge. This sat uneasily with the Anglo-Irish literary revival, led by an elitist group of southern Protestants, seeking to come to terms with their Irishness and occupying a marginal position on the fringe of the cultural nationalist developent. Clearly then, cultural nationalism emerged in the 1890s for a complex series of reasons, and this partly explains the tensions that surfaced within the movement in the early years of the twentieth century.

Of course, cultural nationalism did not begin with the Gaelic revival of the late nineteenth century. Indeed, many of the leading figures in the revival drew inspiration from the activities of the Young Irelanders who had sought to blend culture and politics in the 1840s. There were obvious parallels, because many of the Young Ireland writers were responding to the increased Anglicisation in Irish life in pre-famine Ireland. This intellectual backlash was led by Thomas Davis, who focused on Ireland's separate culture, language and race in highlighting the differences between Britain and Ireland. Of course, Davis was not the first Protestant to take an interest in Ireland's cultural heritage. Such interest had been particularly evident among elements of the Ascendancy class in the late eighteenth century, but Davis attached a clear political dimension to his cultural nationalism. Like many of his Young Ireland colleagues, Davis was uncomfortable with what he regarded as the narrow sectarian nationalism advocated by O'Connell. Clearly influenced by contemporary European developments, Davis articulated a romantic view of nationalism that emphasised the unity of all Irishmen, irrespective of their religion or class. His aim was to build a common sense of nationality among all Irishmen, which would be clearly rooted in the past. But Davis could not turn back the clock, and his thinking glossed over the very real religious and political difficulties which the more practical O'Connell fully appreciated. Though he denied it, Davis's view of Irish nationality was an elitist one, but this can be partially explained by his religion. With O'Connell making effective use of Catholic numbers, the only way for Protestants such as Davis to retain positions of leadership in Irish political life was through cultural nationalism.

Davis's death in September 1845, the subsequent Young Ireland drift into revolutionary nationalism, and the impact of the famine combined to sweep cultural nationalism off the political map. Yet Davis had left a deep imprint. While his call for the unity of Irishmen went unheeded, his belief that Ireland's distinct culture was the basis of Irish nationality provided the prop for cultural nationalists at the turn of the century. Yet cultural nationalism did not disappear entirely in the post-famine period. The Phoenix Society, founded in Skibbereen in 1856 by O'Donovan Rossa, was the best-known of a number of literary societies operating in County Cork. Attracting the shopkeepers, clerks and artisans from the ranks of the petty bourgeoisie, these clubs provided a forum for the discussion of advanced nationalist ideas, though they were soon to be swallowed up by the Fenian movement. Yet there was also a definite overlap from the Young Ireland days, and the Phoenix Societies kept alive the new approach to nationalism offered by Davis. There was considerable interest in the language and in Gaelic culture, as these small groups of men sought to rationalise their opposition to English rule. Later, a small group of literary Fenians, most notably Charles J Kickham, produced a series of patriotic ballads and novels which enjoyed a wide readership among later generations of nationalists. Kickham's work looked back to a purer, simplified past, which elevated the landless labourer to hero status and firmly rejected the drift to commercialisation in rural Ireland.

Further evidence that there was an upsurge of nostalgia in rural Ireland and support for a new approach, which developed a separate expression of identity, came in 1884 with the launch of the Gaelic Athletic Association (GAA). Its founder, Michael Cusack, a teacher and sports enthusiast, had become convinced that the spread of English games such as rugby and cricket was having a detrimental effect on national morale. The aim of the GAA was to promote Irish sports and, from the outset, the movement enjoyed the full backing of Dr TW Croke, the Archbishop of Cashel, who was an outspoken critic of English cultural advances in Ireland. Whereas Croke was an enthusiastic and committed supporter of the GAA, many clerics were initially hesitant about endorsing a movement which, it was feared, could become a rival to the Church in rural Ireland. Very soon, however, the clergy recognised the popularity of a movement which provided new opportunities for organised recreational activity. Within five years of its formation it had 50,000 members, and the competitive element, which saw matches arranged between local parishes, ensured that the GAA contributed to the development of local patriotism. At national level the organisation of inter-county competitions saw the GAA play its part in the rapid growth of organised spectator sport, which was such a feature of the social history of the British Isles before World War One.

Although it was essentially a cultural and sporting body, the GAA attracted its share of political interest. From the outset the movement secured considerable Fenian support. Adopting the policy of infiltrating suitable open nationalist organisations, the Fenian movement dominated the GAA's ruling executive within three years of its formation. This development provoked renewed hostility from sections of the

Catholic Church, and this was intensified when the GAA threw its support behind Parnell during the split of 1890–91. As a result, membership declined during the 1890s, but this trend was reversed when the movement was reorganised, with clerical backing, though with continued Fenian involvement, at the beginning of the twentieth century. Yet on its formation the GAA also won the backing of many prominent figures within constitutional nationalism, and it clearly benefited from the national self-confidence which Parnellism had bestowed on rural Ireland. Moreover, in its promotion of traditional Irish sports and its opposition to English games, the GAA could not avoid political controversy, and this gave militants within the movement repeated opportunities to articulate anti-English sentiment. In this way the GAA made an early contribution to the revival of national feeling in rural Ireland.

While the GAA found an eager audience in the Irish countryside for its blend of cultural and sporting activities, a literary renaissance was taking place in much grander surroundings. In 1885 Charles Oldham and TW Rolleston, both graduates of Trinity College, established the *Dublin University Review*, which provided a platform for those aspiring to a higher form of culture. The most notable figure in this Anglo-Irish literary revival was William Butler Yeats who established the Irish Literary Society of London in December 1891 and followed this with the launch of the National Literary Society in Dublin in May 1892. Writing in English, but drawing their inspiration from ancient Celtic myths and legends, Yeats and his followers sought to promote a more subtle sense of Irish identity that would stress an inclusive culture. For this, Davis provided the inspiration. In his work Yeats focused on themes that highlighted Ireland's separate cultural identity and, though Davis had stressed the importance of the Irish language, his mind was open to the notion that this new sense of Irishness could also be expressed in the English language. After Davis, Yeats looked for inspiration to two other celebrated figures, Standish O'Grady and Samuel Ferguson. Though Protestants like Davis, O'Grady and Ferguson were opposed to political nationalism, but their keen sense of Irishness, combined with their outstanding literary talent, built a strong base for the next generation of cultural nationalists. Moreover, the non-sectarian nature of their work, which first popularised Celtic mythology, appealed to Yeats. These men were proud to be Irishmen but were also proud of their Protestantism, and they were committed to the belief that Ireland needed Protestant leadership. Yeats, of course, was from a landed gentry family in Sligo and he, too, was anxious that members of his caste would continue to assume positions of influence in a future nationalist, democratic Ireland.

It was the success of Parnellism in the 1880s which first encouraged Yeats and his fellow Anglo-Irish patriots to engage in the literary movement. Later, the death of Parnell and the subsequent petty squabbling of his former parliamentary colleagues were taken by Yeats and his followers as a signal to press the cultural alternative more aggressively. The role played by the Catholic Church during the split had increased the pressure on these patriotic intellectuals to develop their notion of inclusivity within the literary revival. Yet this was a forlorn hope. The literary revival struggled to break out of its tiny elitist circle and appeal to the mass of Irishmen. Yeats's associates – JM Synge, Lady Gregory, George Russell (AE), Edward Martyn and George Moore – took their inspiration from the ordinary people, but they were reluctant to come off their intellectual pedestals. They saw themselves as the artists of the national movement, engaged in the production of a new literature for an evolving country, and, though they recognised that they were a tiny minority, they played a crucial role in raising awareness of a distinct Irish culture.

It was another of Yeats's colleagues in the National Literary Society who succeeded in giving cultural nationalism a broader appeal. Douglas Hyde was the son of a Church of Ireland clergyman and he played a pivotal role in the Gaelic revival. Before going to Trinity College, Hyde had grown up in Frenchpark, County Roscommon, where he learned about Ireland's rich Gaelic heritage from local people speaking in their native language. Hyde wished to spark a revival of the Irish language, but he was also closely linked to Yeats and his circle of Anglo-Irish intellectuals. It was Hyde's inaugural lecture as President of the National Literary Society, delivered in November 1892, which provided the inspiration for the language revival in the 1890s. 'The Necessity for De-anglicising the Irish People' demanded immediate action to halt the decline of the language and then denounced the imitation of English manners and customs. The lecture also set out Hyde's vision of a cultural revival which would be non-sectarian and non-political. This would, of course, encourage his fellow Protestants to play a full role in the language movement and, in articulating this notion of a cultural revival which would be above politics, Hyde was echoing the views expressed by Yeats.

Hyde's lecture had reawakened interest in the language movement and had encouraged a young Dublin clerk, Eoin MacNeill, to establish a new organisation. Previously, both the Society for the Preservation of the Irish Language, formed in 1876, and the Gaelic Union, formed in 1880, had campaigned for the greater use of the Irish language, but while they enjoyed a degree of success, their appeal was extremely narrow. MacNeill's new movement, the Gaelic League, which was established in July 1893, sought to revive Irish as a spoken and literary language. MacNeill had come from an Ulster Catholic middle-class background and, like Hyde, had not been a native Irish speaker but had learned the language in an attempt to discover his own cultural roots.

While working in Dublin, MacNeill had also carried out meticulous research into Ireland's Gaelic past. Indeed, his academic achievements saw him appointed to the first chair of Early and Medieval Irish History at University College Dublin in 1909. The third key figure in the formation of the Gaelic League was Father Eugene O'Growney, the Professor of Irish at Maynooth. These three, a southern Catholic, a northern Catholic and a southern Protestant, stood at the head of the Gaelic League, and their varied religious and geographical backgrounds appeared to confirm Hyde's vision that the language would provide "a mental field upon which all Irishmen might meet". Although MacNeill shared many of Hyde's ideas, he was less willing to acknowledge the contributions of the mainly Protestant writers to the cause of Irish nationality, preferring to identify its roots in the remote Gaelic past. Moreover, in his desire to establish the Gaelic League as a truly popular movement, the more practical MacNeill assumed that this would require close collaboration with sympathetic elements of the Catholic clergy who had come under O'Growney's influence during their training at Maynooth.

The Gaelic League was to become the most important of the various movements engaged in cultural nationalism. Its nurturing of a national identity based exclusively on Gaelic culture and its emphasis on the revival of the Irish language distinguished the League from its more elitist predecessors. But the task of arresting the decline of the language was an extremely difficult one. The use of Irish had been in decline since the middle of the eighteenth century and, by 1801, only 50 per cent of the people spoke monolingual Irish. Its decline in the nineteenth century was spectacular. The impact of the famine greatly accelerated the trend, as the areas which suffered most were those same areas in the poorer parts of the west where Irish was most commonly spoken. By 1851 only 5 per cent of the population spoke monolingual Irish and over the next 50 years this figure dropped to 0.5 per cent. Even the number of bilingual speakers, those who spoke both Irish and English, was down to 14 per cent by the end of the nineteenth century. These figures emphasised the enormity of the task facing the Gaelic League. Indeed, its initial impact was disappointing. By 1897 only 43 branches had been established, as the League found it difficult to translate MacNeill's desire for a popular movement into reality. Certainly, Hyde proved his brilliance as a propagandist, and the League raised its profile by successfully campaigning for letters and parcels addressed in Irish to be accepted by the Post Office, and for bilingual street names and signposts to be accepted by Dublin Corporation. Yet these changes were merely cosmetic. If the language were to enjoy a sustained revival, the League would have to campaign successfully for Irish to become a compulsory subject in the school curriculum.

Initially, the League directed its efforts towards the organisation of weekend literacy camps, the establishment of Gaelic journals and the publication of Irish literature. Only a section of the educated middle class was attracted by the League's programme in this formative period. These included a small but significant number of Protestant enthusiasts, though the majority of the early activists were respectable suburbanites who could be described as members of the Catholic intelligentsia. While they regarded themselves as above politics, their rejection of English economic and cultural influences carried unmistakable political undertones. Although their numbers were small, the energy and ability of the leadership laid secure foundations for future growth. By the end of the century interest in the League had increased sharply and, by 1901, the number of branches had risen to 100. It continued to expand in the early years of the twentieth century and, by 1904, the League had 600 branches with a total membership of approximately 50,000.

This rapid rise in membership was attributable to a number of factors which were to stimulate all forms of nationalism. Firstly, the centenary celebrations of the 1798 rebellion had stirred nationalist passions and benefited constitutional, cultural and revolutionary nationalism. Then, more significantly, the outbreak of the Boer War in October 1899 raised national feeling in Ireland, as all shades of nationalist opinion identified with the Boers in their struggle for independence against the might of the British Empire. The South African War had been a crucial factor in the reunification of the IPP, and many Irish MPs, notably John Dillon, took a passionate interest in the conflict. The conflict in South Africa had raised Irish national consciousness to a new level, and the consequent upsurge in anti-imperialist and anti-English feeling also aroused interest in cultural nationalism.

Therefore, while the death of Parnell and the subsequent schism within constitutional nationalism clearly boosted the cultural revival, and the Gaelic League in particular, its advance at the end of the nineteenth century was not due to further problems for the IPP. In fact, domestic and international events had combined to improve the prospects for all shades of nationalism, and reaction to the Boer War had stimulated cultural nationalism and political nationalism in equal measure. The numbers in the Gaelic League were now swollen by an influx from the ranks of the petty bourgeoisie, as clerks, shop assistants, civil servants and schoolmasters became interested in their cultural past. Another attraction was recreation. The League organised various social gatherings and pastimes which allowed its petty bourgeois members to engage with their own class and exclude all undesirables. Schoolmasters, in particular, played a prominent role in the growth of the League. While they frequently assumed the role of community leader, many of them felt insecure, underpaid and, consequently, discontented. For such people the League provided an outlet for their frustration and ambition. Schoolmasters were also very influential, and many pupils later recalled how their teachers indoctrinated them into radical nationalism. Moreover, teachers normally made the local schoolhouse available for evening language classes, which they themselves frequently conducted. In this they collaborated closely with the local clergy, as the priest often acted as the clerical manager of the local national school, and this increased clerical participation and further encouraged the growth of the League. By the turn of the century an increasing number of clergy had come to regard the Gaelic League as the best buffer against English popular culture, which was threatening to secularise Irish society and undermine the hegemony of the Catholic Church. In rural areas farmers' sons joined the local Gaelic League branch, but the movement was essentially an urban one. The irony was that the League never aroused anything like the same interest in the more remote Irish-speaking areas of the west.

A significant proportion of the new Gaelic League recruits were former emigrants who had recently returned to Ireland. Less inhibited by deference, the broader experience gained by such people had increased their self-confidence and made them more willing to challenge the status quo. For them the Gaelic League proved a more attractive and exciting prospect than the outwardly conservative IPP. Indeed, the majority of League activists were young, educated white-collar workers, many of whom were employed by the state, challenging an older middle class which was frustrating their political and social ambitions. Furthermore, this younger element demonstrated intellectual ambition, much of which was probably pretentious but nevertheless significant, and the League offered the opportunity for self-improvement and the realisation of this intellectual ambition. At the same time, these urban intellectuals were often scornful of the trappings of capitalist society, and they became fascinated by a romantic vision of an idealised Gaelic past which was more egalitarian, viewing the simple life of the poor man as virtuous and fulfilling. Although similar political movements, which were romantic and visionary, were attracting the petty bourgeoisie in a new era of increasing democracy across Europe, the attack on materialism in Ireland became indistinguishable from an attack on Englishness itself. At the popular level, moreover, the Gaelic League increasingly defined Irish nationality in a negative manner by rejecting English influences and values.

If its growth around the turn of the century caused the League to become more political, it also made it more Catholic. This, in turn, made it less attractive to Protestants and a number, who had been active since the movement's formation, left the League. Through its official newspaper *An Claidheamh Soluis* (The Sword of Light), which was launched on 17 March 1899, the League engaged in a highly publicised series of clashes with the Provost of Trinity College, JP Mahaffy, who wanted Irish taken off the intermediate school syllabus. Mahaffy was also critical of the Catholic clergy's interference at lower levels, and the League's rebuttal of his arguments raised public awareness of its work. The League attracted further attention when it campaigned successfully to have St Patrick's Day recognised as a national holiday. More significantly, the League won the right in 1909 to have Irish accepted as a compulsory subject for matriculation in the new National University. Hyde had led the campaign for compulsory Irish, and this threw the League into conflict with the IPP and John Dillon who led the fight against compulsion. The mass membership, which such campaigns had helped to attract, was clearly more Catholic and more concerned with populist values.

The link between the Gaelic revival and Catholicism was most clearly articulated by DP Moran. A gifted journalist,

Moran spent ten years working in London where he joined the city's Gaelic League branch. Returning to Ireland, Moran founded the Dublin weekly newspaper, the *Leader*, which first appeared in September 1900 and became an instant success. Moran conveyed his personal disgust at the level to which Irish society had sunk, and he blamed the spread of English culture for the spate of gambling, drunkenness and immoral literature now destroying Ireland. Moran wanted to foster the language revival, but he warned against a preoccupation with Ireland's Gaelic past, arguing the case for a modern, competitive society on Irish terms. In declaring his vision of an 'Irish Ireland', a phrase that he coined, Moran viciously attacked the IPP, which he accused of negligence in its failure to protect Irish society against English cultural encroachments. In addition to his sustained assault on constitutional nationalism, Moran frequently attacked the separatist tradition and castigated Fenianism as an irrelevance. Not surprisingly, Moran's Irish Ireland philosophy also led him into conflict with the Anglo-Irish literary clique. In his writing Moran dismissed the work of Yeats and his circle as a fraud, arguing that while it may have been Anglo-Irish, it was not Irish. Along with Lady Gregory, George Moore and Edward Martyn, Yeats had founded the Irish Literary Theatre (subsequently the Abbey) in 1898. Their aim was to provide an opportunity for the creative figures in the literary renaissance to develop the Celtic theme in their work and take it to a wider audience. In this venture they were hounded at every turn by Moran who mocked the 'sham patriotism' of their work, describing it as 'un-Irish'. Relations between the Irish Ireland and Anglo-Irish camps hit an all-time low in 1907 with the production of Synge's play *The Playboy of the Western World* at the Abbey. The play, in which a youth who kills his domineering father and then becomes the centre of attention for the local young maidens, reflected the generational tension in contemporary Irish society, but the *Leader* denounced it as 'pagan'. On its first night outraged Irish Irelanders shouted down the actors, and the 'Abbey riots' continued for a full week.

But Moran's articles also carried a crude sectarian message. Nationalism and Catholicism were, for him, inseparable. Therefore, in spite of all his efforts, Yeats could not, in Moran's view, be truly Irish. He and his literary colleagues were denounced as 'West Britons', and the literary renaissance element of the Gaelic revival was effectively marginalised. Labelling Protestants as 'sourfaces', Moran accused them of discrimination against Catholics in employment and of diluting Irish nationalism in politics. Arguing that 'the Irish nation is de facto a Catholic nation', Moran rejected the nationalist claims of the Ascendancy class, as he urged Catholics to make use of their numbers and assert their supremacy. This notion of a narrow, negative, but self-sufficient and fully independent, nationalism ran counter to the inclusive nationalism envisaged by Hyde. While Moran praised the Gaelic League for providing an Irish Ireland alternative to English culture, he insisted that it, by itself, would never create the modern Irish nation which he desired. Moran's answer was to target the growing Catholic urban middle class and link their interest in cultural revival to achievable economic goals. Through their leadership Ireland would be transformed into a modern, self-sufficient, urban society, in which Irishmen would have developed the capacity to think and act as Irishmen. Privately, Hyde agreed with much of Moran's argument, though he recoiled from the populist tone of many of his articles. Moreover, the personalised nature of Moran's attacks often aroused controversy but, as an astute businessman with an eye on the *Leader*'s circulation figures, this was surprising. In truth, Moran was simply articulating the logic of an Irish Ireland view of nationalism. Gaelic culture was, for Moran, the culture of the Irish Catholic, and the Irish nation was a

Catholic nation. Those Protestants who wished to identify with the Irish nation had to recognise this.

Therefore, the rapid growth of the Gaelic League around the turn of the century saw it acquire a clear political dimension which Moran and the *Leader* helped to foster. The cultural revival in general, and the Gaelic League in particular, became more closely identified with Catholicism, and the clergy took a more prominent role. Of course, within the broader sweep of new nationalism there were other small pressure groups that were more political in character. The Gaelic revival had encouraged the participation of a small but active Irish feminist movement. A Belfast based journal, *Shan Van Vocht* (The Poor Old Woman), had been established in 1896 by the Protestant Alice Milligan and her Catholic associate Anna Johnston, both of whom were prominent Gaelic Leaguers in Ulster. The journal produced a series of literary and historical articles but also promoted separatist ideas. When *Shan Van Vocht* ceased publication in 1899, its two founders cooperated with Arthur Griffith, another able journalist, who founded a new newspaper, the *United Irishman*. Griffith was a supporter of both the GAA and the Gaelic League, but his primary interest was in politics where he hoped that the IPP would give way to a more radical, separatist party. Drawing on political and economic ideas popular in contemporary Europe, Griffith established Sinn Fein (Ourselves) in 1905 to act as a rallying point for a variety of tiny radical nationalist groups, many of which had been spawned by the Boer War. One of the groups it incorporated was Inghinidhe na hEireann (The Daughters of Ireland), a more overtly political feminist organisation founded by Maud Gonne in 1900. In all of these organisations there was a considerable overlap of membership, with the Gaelic League retaining its dominant position.

The impact made by the League and the cluster of organisations labouring under the cultural nationalist umbrella must not obscure the fact that, in terms of numbers, cultural nationalism was very much a minority movement. The UIL had more members than the Gaelic League, and while the IPP never recaptured the energy and dynamism of the early 1880s, it remained an efficient political force enjoying the support of the vast majority of Irish nationalists. Indeed, the return of a Liberal government in 1906 gave a further boost to the IPP just at the point when the rise of cultural nationalism appeared to have peaked. Even the embryonic Irish labour movement stood comparison with cultural nationalism, as the Irish Trades Union Congress represented 60,000 workers by 1900. Of course, the role played by former Gaelic League activists in the 1916 Easter Rising conferred a retrospective significance on the movement. It is true that individual IRB members, particularly in Munster, joined the League soon after its formation, but the IRB only gained control of the movement in 1915. By that stage the League had become explicitly nationalist under the influence of these separatist infiltrators, and Hyde had resigned in protest. From the outset Hyde had wanted the League to stay aloof from politics and he was adamant that it would not be attached to any political party. In this way it developed as a romantic and visionary movement that was anti-parliamentary in character. Yet, in spite of Hyde's protestations, it was clear that a movement inspired by nationalism would have to be political. In Irish society, moreover, where nationalism was such a pervasive influence, the Gaelic League was unlikely to escape its political clutches. It was left to Moran to administer a weekly dose of realism in the *Leader*.

In analysing the nature of cultural nationalism a number of historians have recently emphasised that the cultural revival was concerned with the 'invention of tradition', rather than the defence of a strong existing culture. Hence, it can be argued that both the GAA and the Gaelic League were movements engaged in the creation of a separate Irish culture. Moreover, a comparison with the Welsh experience throws interesting light on the relationship between culture and politics. At the end of the nineteenth century cultural nationalism was a prominent feature of Welsh society and the use of the native language was much more widespread than in Ireland. In spite of the clear presence of a strong Welsh identity, there was no consequent rise in Welsh political nationalism. The Welsh were proud of their language and culture, but they were happy to remain part of the United Kingdom. In Ireland, by contrast, political separatism developed out of cultural nationalism.

6

Defenders of the Union

BY THE END OF THE nineteenth century Catholic nationalism had asserted itself as the dominant political force in Ireland. It had been transformed by the electoral changes of the 1880s and by the emergence of a confident, middle-class leadership. Mirroring this development, as the century progressed, the defence of the Union became increasingly associated with the Protestant interest. Yet this was a reversal of the pattern at the time the Union was enacted. Its most implacable opponents in 1799–1800 had been those members of the Protestant Ascendancy who refused to waver in the face of financial inducements and political pressure from Westminster. At the time these men rejected Lord Clare's central argument that only the Union could provide an effective defence for the Irish Protestant nation. However, this sentiment did not last. While the Anglo-Irish opponents of the Union were proud of the Irish nation and proud of their Irishness, they soon realised that it was pointless to continue the struggle and they quickly reconciled themselves to the Union, knowing that there was no prospect of reversing the decision. Indeed, little changed in the years after the Union. The Irish Parliament had gone, but Protestant fears over concessions to Catholics did not materialise. The Ascendancy class, in general, began to appreciate Pitt's argument that they would be more secure as a majority in the United Kingdom than they would as a minority in Ireland. The price of this security, of course, was the surrender of power to

Westminster.

Catholics, on the other hand, had mixed views on the Union. While O'Connell and the small group of Catholic lawyers had opposed the Union from the start, other Catholic elements, notably the Church, had given the measure some degree of support, convinced that the new constitutional arrangement was preferable to the Irish Parliament. This optimism, however, quickly dissipated. Having failed to overcome opposition from both English and Irish Protestants, Westminster could not meet Catholic aspirations. Consequently, Catholic resentment grew and this culminated in a sustained demand for the return of an Irish parliament in Dublin, as Catholics increasingly blamed the Union for all of their social, economic and political grievances. In this way religion became a key component of Irish nationalism. With Protestants uniting to defend the Union, political division in nineteenth century Ireland was characterised by a clear sectarian division. While there was, of course, some deviation in both religious camps, it was never sufficient to alter the pattern which was established in Irish politics during the nineteenth century.

The greatest influence on the development of Protestant politics in the first half of the nineteenth century was Daniel O'Connell. Under his leadership Catholics united and organised efficiently to make use of their numerical superiority. In the 1820s and 1830s O'Connell effectively broke the landlords' control over their tenants at elections, as he mobilised the Catholic population in the successful campaign for Catholic emancipation. His fiercest critics had been the Irish Tories who had consistently opposed Catholic concessions since the 1790s. In the years immediately after the Union, these same Tories had thwarted Pitt's attempts to carry emancipation, but the formation of the Catholic Association in 1823 presented a new challenge for Irish Toryism. In creating the Catholic political nation, O'Connell inadvertently contributed to the development of a new Protestant political consciousness. Moreover, Irish Tories learned the art of party organisation directly from O'Connell. An Irish Protestant Conservative Society was formed in 1831, shortly before a general election and in preparation for the changes envisaged in the Great Reform Act of 1832. This body monitored the work of local registration clubs whose concern was to maximise the Tory vote in all elections. Again following O'Connell's example, these clubs were often controlled by members of the Protestant clergy who regularly resorted to unscrupulous methods in their eagerness to register Tory supporters. Still, in spite of a restricted franchise that favoured property at the expensive of Catholic numbers, the O'Connellites won 39 seats to 30 seats won by the Tories in the general election of 1832. Clearly, Irish Toryism needed a broader appeal as O'Connell turned his fire on the Union itself. In 1836 the Irish Protestant Conservative Society gave way to the Irish Metropolitan Conservative Society, a more moderate body reflecting the changes that Peel had introduced to English Conservatism in his attempt to modernise the party and capture the popular vote. In the following year's general election more efficient organisation and extra funds led to Tory victories in 34 seats, and this figure climbed to 40 in the 1841 general election.

In demonstrating their electoral ability, the Irish Tories had frustrated the anticipated domination of the O'Connellite party. Indeed, in the euphoria of the emancipation triumph, O'Connell himself had confidently predicted the collapse of Irish Toryism, or the "Orange party", a term which he used frequently to describe his electoral opponents. The Orange Order was a Protestant political society which spread quickly from its south Ulster base at the end of the eighteenth century. With a reputation for extremism and aggression, the Order was initially boycotted by most of the landowning class, but O'Connell's success in the 1820s and the growing threat of Catholic power brought a change in outlook. In spite of its volatile nature, Irish Tories recognised the Order's political potential, and the relationship between Toryism and Orangeism improved significantly in the late 1820s, as increasing numbers of the gentry class joined the Order. By this stage its membership approached 100,000. The Orange Order was a direct consequence of the rising sectarian disorder in south Ulster, particularly in County Armagh, where clashes between the rival factions increased sharply in the 1790s. Of course sectarian bitterness had a long history in this area, but, towards the end of the eighteenth century, fierce economic competition between the two religious groups added a new dimension to the problem. Armagh was the most densely populated county in Ireland, and competition for land was fierce, as farmer-weavers on both sides of the religious divide fought for their share of the lucrative linen trade. The result was a series of violent clashes, culminating in a mini-battle at the Diamond near Loughgall in September 1795. Following their victory the Protestants marched to Loughgall, where they formally established the Orange Order. Soon, the Order was associated with the bloody suppression of the 1798 rebellion and was drawn into politics by the impending Act of Union. On balance, the Orange Order opposed the Union. It regarded the Irish Parliament as the best defence of Irish Protestant interests, and it was convinced that the Union would lead to Catholic emancipation.

However, the success of O'Connellism transformed Orange thinking on the Union. Activists within the movement were drawn towards Irish Toryism and the Order played a prominent role in its support for Conservative candidates during election periods. Although it had become increasingly involved in mainstream politics, the Order could not shed its violent image. Frequently, its actions created unwelcome publicity and, in spite of its obvious loyalty to the British Crown, successive Westminster governments regarded it as a threat to public order and sought to weaken its influence. In 1825 it was temporarily suppressed, along with the Catholic Association, but was soon revived. Then, in 1836, following a highly critical parliamentary report which uncovered evidence of deliberate Orange infiltration in both the yeomanry and the army, the Order was formally dissolved. Thereafter, it survived in semi-underground fashion and continued to exercise influence at local level, where it occasionally orchestrated violent sectarian clashes. By the mid-1840s the movement had been revived, and it quickly renewed its links with Irish Toryism.

By this stage its reputation had again reduced the numbers of participating gentry, but it was significant that it had acquired a substantial Presbyterian membership in the north. This was important, because the vast majority of the Order's early members were Church of Ireland, but, by the 1830s, the Episcopalians and Presbyterians in Ulster had moved closer together. The key figure in this development was the Reverend Henry Cooke, a Presbyterian cleric from County Down. Cooke had been engaged in a fierce theological struggle with the liberal wing of Presbyterianism, which was led by the Reverend Henry Montgomery. By the late 1820s Cooke's conservative faction was in the ascendant and, following his victory over Montgomery, he became publicly associated with Irish Toryism. In October 1834, in an address to an O'Connell-style monster meeting, he told 40,000 Protestants gathered at Hillsborough, County Down, that Protestants had to overcome their denominational differences and learn to work together to combat the growing Catholic threat.

While Cooke never persuaded a majority of Presbyterians to ally with Irish Conservatism, he did succeed in exploiting

Protestant fears of Catholicism and undoubtedly contributed to the formation of a Protestant political consciousness. Moreover, he did not steer Ulster Presbyterians away from radical politics. They had become disillusioned in the immediate aftermath of the 1798 rebellion, and they particularly distrusted O'Connell and his Catholic agenda. Cooke articulated these fears and he spoke for the vast majority of Presbyterians in his opposition to O'Connell's repeal movement. He frequently led the response to O'Connell's anti-Protestant rhetoric and organised the opposition to O'Connell's Belfast visit in 1841. At the subsequent Conservative celebrations Cooke's speech highlighted the economic success of Belfast, arguing that future prosperity depended on the Union. Although most Presbyterians continued to support the Liberal party in the mid-nineteenth century, Cooke's efforts had made Irish Toryism, hitherto anathema, respectable in Ulster Presbyterian eyes. In promoting the Irish Conservative cause, Cooke also maintained close links with English Conservatism and his influence helped to draw Irish and English Conservatism closer together. For Cooke this was a natural process and it countered the alliance between O'Connellite nationalism and the Whig party in Britain. In this way Cooke helped to lay the foundation for the future link between Irish unionism and the British Conservative party.

The increasing prosperity of Belfast, to which Cooke had alluded in 1841, strengthened the case for the defence of the Union. The city grew even more quickly in the second half of the nineteenth century as the introduction of engineering and shipbuilding added to the established textile industry. Booming industrial expansion attracted thousands of prospective workers eager to improve their economic lot and escape from the endless cycle of rural poverty. In the middle of the nineteenth century this urban migration was disproportionately Catholic. In 1800 an estimated 10 per cent of Belfast's 20,000 population was Catholic, but, by the census of 1861, 34 per cent of Belfast's 121,000 population was Catholic. The increasing prosperity of Belfast in the mid-nineteenth century coincided with the fatal collapse of the Irish rural economy and, as Catholics occupied the least secure position in rural Ulster, the famine surely increased the trend of Catholic urban migration. For their protection each religious community tended to live in segregated areas, and it soon became possible to identify both Catholic and Protestant working-class districts of the city. The influx of new workers raised sectarian tension in the city to new levels, and minor incidents occasionally led to serious rioting between the two communities. In 1857, 1864 and 1872 rioting erupted in July with the approach of the 'Twelfth' celebrations and continued for much of the summer, causing serious loss of life and widespread damage.

Key religious and political events in the 1850s and 1860s helped to shape Ulster Protestant politics. Cooke continued to warn of the Catholic threat to Protestant liberties, and the American-imported, great evangelical revival of 1859 brought together Protestants of all denominations, creating a new spiritual consensus and emphasising the differences, political as well as doctrinal, between Protestants and Catholics. At the same time, the Orange Order increased its influence in Belfast's Protestant working-class districts. One of its principal leaders from the early 1860s until the end of the century was William Johnston, a small landowner from Ballykilbeg, County Down. In February 1868 Johnston was given a one-month jail sentence for his role in leading an Orange march in defiance of the Party Processions Act, which was used by the authorities to ban all Orange and other potentially explosive marches between 1850 and 1872. Treated as a martyr by the Belfast Protestant working class, Johnston stood as an independent in Belfast in the general election of November 1868 and trounced his Conservative opponent. Although his victory dismayed the Conservative squires leading the party, they recognised his electoral appeal in the wake of the 1867 Reform Act which enfranchised skilled workers. After his success as an independent he was endorsed as a Conservative party candidate and, following a redistribution, he held the South Belfast seat until his death in 1902. Johnston's rise to prominence was significant, because it marked the beginning of a powerful link between Orange populism and the Conservative party in Ulster.

The leaders of Belfast's thriving business community were predominantly middle-class Presbyterians and, as their primary concern was the establishment of trading links with Britain for their export-oriented businesses, they had little attachment to the rest of Ireland. Of course, local loyalty was powerful in all parts of Ireland, but the Presbyterian bourgeoisie offered a distinct contrast to Ulster's landlords, who were usually members of the Church of Ireland and shared a much greater sense of community with fellow members of their Church in the three southern provinces.

In the second half of the nineteenth century the number of Protestants in Leinster, Munster and Connacht was close to 250,000, or 10 per cent of the total population. This figure included the landed gentry and a large group of urban professionals, particularly in Dublin and Cork, but it also included many shopkeepers, farmers and labourers. For the most part, these southern Protestants were well scattered and it was only in a few isolated areas that they were able to mount a serious electoral challenge with the prospect of victory. Their electoral capacity had been seriously damaged by emancipation and by the various alterations both to the franchise and to the constituency boundaries that had occurred in the middle of the century. Still, they were well organised, and bodies such as the Central Conservative

Society, formed in 1853, were able to seize the few electoral opportunities that presented themselves. Not surprisingly, it was the families of the landed interest who played the dominant role in Conservative politics in the three southern provinces. The key factor in the subsequent organisation of political unionism, the movement to defend the Union, was the alliance of the Ulster bourgeoisie and the Irish landlords, a reversal of their historic antagonism. This alliance was, of course, born out of political necessity, and tension was never far from the surface. On the positive side, however, the alliance enjoyed great social standing, with easy access to British high politics, and real financial muscle. This explains its resilience in the face of the great Home Rule struggles at the end of the nineteenth and beginning of the twentieth centuries.

For Protestants living in southern Ireland the Church of Ireland played a crucial role in providing a focus for scattered, sometimes vulnerable, communities. Indeed, the boost given to the Church by the impact of the evangelical revival had increased the sense of purpose and influence of the established church. Later, in tandem with Irish Toryism, the Church of Ireland mounted a determined, but ultimately unsuccessful, struggle to stop Gladstone's disestablishment plan. Catholic nationalism had long demanded disestablishment, and the 1869 Irish Church Act formed a major plank in Gladstone's new Irish policy initiative. It also coincided, as Gladstone recognised, with a major triumph for Irish Liberals in the general election of 1868, when they won 66 seats. Gladstone was quick to take advantage of what appeared to be a solid Catholic/Presbyterian alliance on the issue of disestablishment. Such a rapprochement was, of course, tactical and temporary, and, in the end, disestablishment removed a major bone of contention between the Church of Ireland and its Presbyterian counterpart. Therefore, disestablishment in 1869 paved the way to greater Protestant unity which, in turn, eased the task of transforming unionism from a political slogan into an organised political movement.

In the 1868 general election a clear pattern was discernible. Members of the Church of Ireland voted Conservative, while Catholics and most northern Presbyterians voted Liberal. At the time, therefore, Irish politics appeared to be an extension of British politics, as the two great parties, Liberal and Conservative, competed for power. The advent of Butt's Home Rule organisation, and its initial success at the 1874 general election, broke this pattern. Constitutional nationalism consolidated its position in the 1880 general election, as Home Rulers were returned in 62 seats, leaving the Conservatives with 26 and the Liberals with 15 seats. Therefore, unionism did not respond immediately to the challenge of Parnellism. At this point the earliest and most energetic element in the unionist cause was the landlord class in all parts of Ireland. Landlords saw the agrarian agitation as a direct threat to their dominant position in Irish society. In addition to this class dimension, landlords also viewed the agitation in sectarian terms. This was particularly true in the north, where the landed interest enlisted the enthusiastic support of the Orange Order which, of course, already had close links with the Conservative party, in countering the land agitation. Although, initially, the Land League enjoyed considerable support among the north's tenant farmers, it was increasingly seen as a nationalist front, and the Orange Order was able to provide a cross-class Protestant alliance to repel the agrarian threat in Ulster. Very soon, the Order was providing a solid organisational base for the development of political unionism, and its ability to paper over class and denominational cracks within Protestantism made it a vital element in the creation of a viable political alternative to nationalism. However, the downside to the Order's involvement was that it limited unionism's appeal outside the Protestant population and, in so doing, reinforced the sectarian nature of Irish politics.

Of course, a crucial factor in the development of both unionism and nationalism was the 1884 Representation of the People Act, which increased the Irish electorate from 224,000 to 738,000. In enfranchising farm labourers and small tenant farmers the legislation boosted constitutional nationalism, which now threatened to take Conservative and Liberal seats in Ulster, where Protestant numbers were concentrated. Indeed, awareness of the growing nationalist threat in the province had already been heightened by Tim Healy's by-election success in North Monaghan in June 1883. Subsequently, nationalists loudly proclaimed that 'the invasion of Ulster' had begun. Again, it was the Orange Order that was first to respond to this nationalist advance, organising a series of counter-demonstrations, including the infamous incident at Rosslea, County Fermanagh, in October 1883, when a large number of troops had to be deployed in order to prevent serious disorder. When a nationalist rally had been planned for the village, the Order quickly called a counter-demonstration, bringing in some 7,000 supporters from neighbouring counties. Shots were fired as the Orangemen, led by Lord Rossmore, refused to have their march re-routed. As tension rose throughout the province, these incidents became more frequent and, naturally, politics became even more polarised.

The obvious determination of nationalists to increase their representation in Ulster, and the changes made to the franchise qualification in 1884, demonstrated the need for Protestant unity. Healy's by-election victory had raised the number of Home Rule MPs in Ulster to three, but it was clear that nationalists would increase this figure substantially at the next general election. The experience of the previous quarter of a century had indicated that the

Conservatives, rather than the Liberals, offered the most effective opposition to the growth of nationalism. It was the Conservative party, therefore, that provided the major influence in the early development of unionism. The Conservatives had already established close links with a reinvigorated Orange Order, and the Order played a crucial role in the general political mobilisation of the 1880s. At the same time, unionism benefited from the emergence of much greater Protestant solidarity and from a general feeling of superiority, which had been evident for most of the century. This gave early Unionists an unshakeable confidence in spite of their numerical disadvantage. The key to the success of unionism would be the remarkable coalition between landed and business interests, both of which regarded the defence of the Union as essential to their future prosperity.

7

The Organisation
of Unionism

UNIONISM, AS AN ORGANISED political movement, dates
from 1885. With a general election expected and
Parnellism threatening to sweep all before it, the Irish
Loyal and Patriotic Union (ILPU) was founded on 1 May
1885. The initiative had been taken by a small group of
southern landowners and academics, whose aim was to
coordinate electoral opposition to Home Rule candidates. The
ILPU sought collaboration between Conservatives and
Liberals in the southern provinces and offered support to any
candidate who pledged himself to defend the Union. Still, an
indication of the vulnerability felt by pro-Union supporters in
the south was the delay in the public announcement of the
formation of the ILPU until October 1885, one month before
the general election. Indeed, though it was very active in the
election, producing more than 280,000 pamphlets, the
existence of such a hostile political climate meant that much
of its work had to be done discreetly. The ILPU supported 52
candidates in the general election, but there were no
successes. In fact, the only two pro-Union victories in the
south were the two unopposed candidates for Trinity College.
The failure of the ILPU to make any electoral impact was
disappointing, but its supporters were not disillusioned and
their determination to thwart the Home Rule designs of their
lower-class political and religious opponents remained strong.
Its predominantly landed leadership had been alarmed by the

activities of the Land League in the early 1880s, and they feared that a Home Rule parliament, dominated by their enemies, would either force them out directly by confiscating their lands, or indirectly through penal taxation.

After their initial electoral foray the ILPU reassessed its strategy. While the 1885 general election had highlighted the futility of contesting seats in the south, the movement's leaders appreciated that some form of constituency organisation should be developed in order to maintain morale among pro-Union supporters. Two other options remained open and both were tried. The ILPU had many contacts in British politics, and its members could use their influence on the mainland to encourage their parliamentary friends at Westminster to stand firm in the face of nationalist pressure for Home Rule. Another ploy was to develop close cooperation with their allies in Ulster, where there were obvious electoral possibilities. In the northern province, meanwhile, considerable consternation was caused by the announcement of Gladstone's conversion to Home Rule following the general election. The election itself had a sobering effect on the Conservative party in Ulster. It won 16 seats to the 17 won by nationalists. The Liberals were left without any representation, but their participation had undoubtedly cost the Conservatives a number of seats. Gladstone's sudden move and the normal post-election analysis of results had forced opponents of Home Rule to come to terms with their differences. The lead was taken by a number of Conservative landowners who founded the Ulster Loyalist Anti-Repeal Union (ULARU) on 8 January 1886. From the outset the ULARU was active in staging a series of meetings across the province, and it moved quickly to establish close relations with both the Orange Order and the Protestant Churches.

The new movement received a boost from the highly publicised visit of Lord Randolph Churchill to Belfast in February 1886. The ULARU had undertaken much of the organisation for the visit, and Churchill delighted an Ulster Hall audience of Conservatives and Orangemen when he assured them that the Conservative party in Britain would back them in their hour of need. Churchill's sentiments are important, as they marked a symbolic commitment by the Conservative leadership to their Irish cousins in the struggle against Home Rule. Yet in playing 'the Orange card' Churchill was clearly guilty of political opportunism, as his real aim was to exploit Gladstone's conversion to Home Rule and the consequent opposition in Ulster to advance the Conservative cause in Britain.

Indeed, the announcement of Gladstone's support for Home Rule in December 1885, and the subsequent formation of a Liberal government on 30 January 1886, made the introduction of a Home Rule Bill inevitable. It was with this prospect in view that a number of Ulster MPs with Orange connections had come together on 25 January to create a separate Irish Unionist party in Parliament. The inspiration for this move had come from Colonel Edward Saunderson, a County Cavan landlord and leading figure in the Church of Ireland who had represented the county as a Liberal MP from 1865 to 1874. The Land War, however, had altered Saunderson's political views, and he joined the Orange Order in 1882 before being returned as the Conservative MP for North Armagh in 1885. Saunderson was the first leader of Irish unionism and he directed the party's attack on the 1886 Home Rule Bill. Yet Saunderson was a complex character. His Liberal party background saw him eager to promote a non-sectarian unionism, but his passionate commitment to the Orange Order and the recognition of the Order's crucial organisational role for unionism ensured that his wish would never be realised. Ideologically, he believed in a form of Tory paternalism that was based on a landlord-led Protestant alliance. In spite of his obvious Conservative sympathies, Saunderson was convinced that Irish unionism should have its own distinct voice at Westminster. Only by developing this self-reliance and freedom of action, he argued, could the long-term security of loyal Irishmen be protected. In fact, Saunderson had been urging the formation of an independent party at Westminster since the previous year, warning of the Conservative party's lack of concern for loyalists in Ireland. This sense of urgency increased when, in the second half of 1885, it appeared that the Conservatives might opt for an alliance with Parnellism. By introducing his Home Rule Bill, Gladstone had simplified the situation for Saunderson, but he continued to campaign for a strong, independent Irish Unionist voice at Westminster and remained wary of his Conservative allies.

If Gladstone had clarified the position for Saunderson, he had thrown Ulster Liberalism into confusion. On 19 March 1886 a Liberal convention of 600 delegates met in Belfast to discuss recent events and inform Gladstone of their views, but no consensus was reached. However, the introduction of the Home Rule Bill on 8 April finally forced Ulster Liberals to face reality, and the majority decided to join with their old Conservative foes and oppose Home Rule. This was confirmed on 13 April when the Liberal deserters joined Conservatives in a great Ulster Hall protest meeting. Still, this was a bitter pill for many of these former Liberals to swallow and, though they had to acknowledge the weight of Conservative numbers, they struggled hard to retain a distinct identity within the broad Unionist movement. Led by Saunderson, the Irish Unionist MPs gave vague warnings about the outbreak of civil war in Ulster in the event of Home Rule being enacted. In Ulster, meanwhile, rumours were circulating that the Orange Order would raise a paramilitary force to resist Home Rule, and there was wild talk of thousands of men receiving military training. Nationalists never took such threats seriously. They dismissed rumours of armed resistance as fantasy but, though their assessment in the summer of 1886 was probably correct, nationalists made the initial, and fatal, error of underestimating their opponents' determination to resist Home Rule. Following the Home Rule Bill's defeat in June 1886, Gladstone sought to win popular support for his new policy in a general election. In the seven months since the previous election Ulster politics had been transformed. A parliamentary Unionist party had emerged under Saunderson's leadership, and Gladstone's Home Rule gamble had destroyed, with one stroke, the Liberal party in Ireland. In Ulster the Unionists won 17 of the 33 seats, though two of the victorious Unionists were described as Liberal Unionists. The general election of July 1886 had demonstrated that the Union was by far the most important issue in Ulster politics. A clear unionist/nationalist rivalry had been established as Ulster society was increasingly polarised on religious grounds. In fact, the election had been held against a background of serious violence in Belfast. The Home Rule crisis had obviously raised the sectarian temperature and trouble flared in June following a row at the shipyard. The violence continued until September, claiming around 50 lives and ravaging working-class districts in the city.

The Liberal defeat in the 1886 general election and the return of a Conservative government under Lord Salisbury saw the Home Rule danger pass, if only temporarily. Thereafter, Saunderson was impressed by Arthur Balfour's tough security response to agrarian disorder in the south, but he was undoubtedly perturbed by the Conservative government's land legislation, fearing that some form of compulsory purchase might be introduced. This was a concern that he shared with his fellow landlords in the rest of Ireland. While he recognised that the electoral success of unionism depended primarily on Ulster Protestant support, Saunderson viewed the party which he led as an Irish party. Although he sat for North Armagh, his residence in County Cavan allowed Saunderson to empathise with southern gentry living in predominantly nationalist communities. Moreover, his landed and Church of Ireland background meant that he shared essential common interests with the landlord class in the south and west of Ireland. Indeed, it was the challenge faced by these Irish landlords which had a crucial impact in the early development of unionism. Yet the success of the land agitation, which had squeezed concessions from the British government, indicated that the landlord class was in steady decline. This made its alliance with the Ulster bourgeoisie vital to the success of unionism. While this new form of unionism was essentially the creation of the Home Rule crisis, it is wrong to view the movement simply in negative terms. In Parliament its leaders frequently expressed their political beliefs using negative and antagonistic language, particularly in this formative period, but there was more to unionism than the defence of Protestant privilege in Ireland. It had solid foundations, building on the organisation and structure of the Irish Conservative party, and it took advantage of the easing of denominational differences within Protestantism. Maintenance of the Union was seen as essential to future social and economic progress in Ireland. At the same time, unionism benefited from the emergence of a distinct British identity that was, in part, a response to the advance of Catholic nationalism and, more significantly, the result of Ulster's economic development.

The general election results of 1885 and 1886 had highlighted the boundary that existed between north and south. There was, moreover, a difference in emphasis in the cases that southern and northern Unionists presented in their rejection of Home Rule. The isolation and vulnerability felt by southern Unionists, who frequently withdrew to the sanctuary of the 'Big House', accounted for their more reasoned and less aggressive opposition to Home Rule. Southern Unionists were more tolerant of the Catholic religion, often because their lack of numbers outside Dublin made them much more reliant on local Catholics whom they employed in a variety of occupations. Outside Ulster, Unionists also distanced themselves from some of the wilder, sectarian rhetoric and, not surprisingly, the safeguarding of civil and religious liberties never featured as prominently on the southern Unionist agenda. In fact, southern Unionists were not exclusively Protestant. A small number of Catholic landowners, lawyers and ex-soldiers shared an instinctive conservatism with their southern Protestant neighbours. Such Catholics had done well out of the Union and they were not convinced by the nationalist argument in favour of Home Rule. All of these southern Unionists were much more concerned with the threat that Home Rule posed to Irish society and, more particularly, to their own privileged position. In spite of their lack of numbers, their social standing, which was clearly under fire in the last two decades of the century, instilled a confidence that allowed them to come to terms with their lack of electoral support.

Southern Unionists, however, did enjoy considerable influence at Westminster, where they appeared to have direct access to the corridors of power. In 1886, 116 of the 144 peers with Irish interests had connections with southern unionism, while a small number held parliamentary seats in the south of England. Indeed, southern Unionists were much more closely integrated with British Conservatism than their Ulster colleagues, a situation which owed much to the existence of close family ties between the two groups. Furthermore, a significant number of these more prominent families owned estates in both Ireland and England. In this way southern Unionists shared many of the anxieties felt by British Conservatives when they looked at the likely impact of Home Rule, and they tended to have a broader, less parochial view than their Ulster colleagues. These concerns centred on the damage that the concession of a Home Rule parliament might inflict on the integrity of both the United Kingdom and the

British Empire. An indication of the Conservative party's interest on the issue came with the decision taken in the summer of 1886 to alter the party's name to the Conservative and Unionist party, and the labels 'Unionist' and 'Conservative' became interchangeable. Still, it was evident that the Conservative party's concern for Ireland was more tactical than genuine. Opposition to Home Rule gave Conservatives the opportunity to attack their political opponents and to appeal to the British electorate.

Irish Unionists, particularly those in the south, had also taken a keen interest in British voters. With the knowledge that any Home Rule Bill would have to secure a majority in the House of Commons, southern Unionists, who could make little electoral impact in Ireland, began to target marginal seats in Britain. Salisbury's convincing victory in 1886 had reinforced the idea that the key battleground for the maintenance of the Union was in Britain. From the outset, then, southern Unionists bombarded selected constituencies in Britain with anti-Home Rule propaganda, and they maintained a constant channel of communication with supporters on the mainland. Southern Unionist morale received a further boost with the Parnellite split of 1891. This led to the formation of the Irish Unionist Alliance (IUA) which superseded the ILPU. Again, the landlord class was to the fore. Among Protestants in the south and west, the commercial and professional classes, while they were often sympathetic to the cause, were usually reluctant to become openly involved, fearing that their participation would have a detrimental effect on businesses which were heavily dependent on Catholic custom. The IUA adopted an ambitious programme, hoping to organise constituency branches in the south, with further plans for multiple sub-branches. Early encouragement came from its two successes in St Stephen's Green and South Dublin in the 1892 general election, which, when added to the two Trinity seats, gave the Unionists a total of 23 seats. Soon, however, the

IUA was forced to recognise its limitations and, by 1906, it had abandoned its plans for constituency branches. Though the IUA failed to become a mass party organisation, it played a crucial role in directing the anti-Home Rule campaign in Britain through its London office. Moreover, in spite of their numerical constraints, southern Unionists often played the dominant role within unionism in these formative years. Well funded and efficiently organised, they were first to react to the dangers presented by Parnellism.

At the outset it was the landlord class, stirred by Colonel Saunderson, who organised Unionist forces in Ulster. For these leaders, Ulster Protestants, with the Orange Order in the vanguard, offered the best protection against the rural chaos threatened by nationalist land agitators. Indeed, Irish Unionists were united by the fear that those directing the agitation might soon hold office in a Home Rule administration. There was also broad agreement among Unionists on the contention that Home Rule would never satisfy Irish nationalists. Saunderson and others frequently quoted nationalist leaders when they claimed that Home Rule would push open the door to complete separation. In 1886, however, Ulster Unionists tended to emphasise the religious objection above any other.

In addition to the obvious geographical difference, there was a distinct class difference between the two Unionist groups. This was clearly illustrated at the Ulster Unionist Convention in June 1892. In opposition Gladstone clung to his belief in Home Rule, and the trend of Liberal by-election successes raised the prospect of a new Liberal government. With a general election pending, leading Ulster Unionists were determined to organise a display of defiant opposition to Home Rule in an attempt to influence opinion in Britain. The Convention was a major propaganda success. A great wooden pavilion had been constructed to hold the 12,000 delegates from all over Ulster. The Duke of Abercorn chaired the proceedings, and the 400-strong platform party represented the cream of Ulster society, with prominent landowners and business leaders very much to the fore. Yet the delegates comprised a broad cross-section of Ulster society, with at least one-third being drawn from the tenant farming class. The initiative in organising the Convention had been taken by the ex-Liberal MP, Thomas Sinclair, who now chaired the Ulster Liberal Unionist Association. Sinclair was determined to refute the claim made by Gladstone's Liberal supporters and Irish nationalists that unionism represented the interests of only the small landed elite, desperately clinging to their exalted status in Ireland and guilty of stirring up sectarian feeling in order to defend their privileges. Sinclair's purpose was, therefore, to impress on English opinion that unionism was a broad church, representing a wide variety of interests. It was, of course, this cross-class alliance within Ulster unionism which allowed it to develop as a dynamic political movement capable of mobilising Protestant opinion in the province. Ultimately, this set it apart from southern unionism. Perhaps, not surprisingly, many of the speakers at the Convention tended to emphasise Ulster resistance to Home Rule, even though there were frequent references to the all-Ireland nature of unionism. Interestingly, it was also evident that the majority of the speeches were moderate and measured in content, suggesting that the enactment of Home Rule would provoke a huge passive resistance campaign in the province, rather than anything approaching civil war. Although Ulster unionism had, from the outset, a distinct militant style, something which was particularly evident in the period before World War One, the reality did not match the rhetoric.

In these early years, however, the focus of Unionist opposition to Home Rule was parliamentary. Gladstone had, as Unionists feared, triumphed in the general election of July 1892. Ireland remained his burning passion, and it was the unfinished business of pacifying Ireland that justified the ageing leader's decision to continue at the head of the Liberal party. Gladstone had responded to the demonstration of defiance at the Convention by arguing that Unionists, who rejected the democratic wishes of a majority of the Irish people, were being unreasonable. As the Liberals were dependent on the IPP to give them an overall majority, it was inevitable that a second Home Rule Bill would follow. When it was introduced in February 1893, there was a flurry of activity among Unionists. In Ulster an attempt was made to mobilise grass-roots supporters, and various organisations, particularly the Ulster Defence Union, were established. In addition, the Conservative party again tapped into anti-Home Rule feeling in Ulster, and a succession of Tory luminaries, including Arthur Balfour, Joseph Chamberlain, the Duke of Devonshire and Lord Salisbury himself, crossed to the province in a repeat of Churchill's 1886 visit to remind Ulster Unionists that the Conservative party would not desert them in their hour of need. Significantly, these morale-boosting visits frequently included speaking engagements in Dublin, where large audiences of Unionist supporters could be guaranteed. In Parliament, meanwhile, the debates on the second Home Rule Bill generated fierce rivalry. These debates dragged on for more than 80 days, as Saunderson and his Unionist colleagues took a leaf out of Parnell's book and resorted to delaying tactics whenever possible. Saunderson was also at the centre of the famous Commons' incident on 27 July 1893, when proceedings had to be suspended following an unsightly brawl in the chamber. The fact that this shocked many Conservatives did not perturb the Unionist leader. In his long experience of challenging Parnell, Saunderson had clearly been influenced by Parnell's leadership style and tactics, and he showed little regard for the negative impact that Unionist excesses might have on Conservative support in Britain.

Unionists, particularly in Ulster, celebrated the outright rejection of the second Home Rule Bill by the House of Lords as an outstanding triumph. Gladstone retired in March 1894 and, with his successor, Lord Rosebery, determined to avoid further Home Rule controversy, Unionists could breathe easily. The subsequent Conservative victory in the general election of July 1895 reinforced this new sense of security. In the process of thwarting Gladstone's Home Rule ambitions, a number of important differences had emerged between supporters of the Union in Ulster, the rest of Ireland and Britain. Occasionally, these tensions would surface, but the Unionist alliance maintained a united front until the second decade of the twentieth century. By the time of the second Home Rule Bill Ulster Unionists had developed a powerful regional identity, though they were perfectly content to work within the broad Irish Unionist front. The role played by the landed leadership was crucial to this. More than other Unionists, the gentry class regarded themselves as Irish. Yet, from 1886 onwards, the bourgeoisie was gradually eroding the power of the landlords within unionism. In 1886 landlords held 50 per cent of the Unionist seats, but this figure had fallen to 33 per cent by 1900, and would fall further. As the bourgeoisie, domiciled primarily in north-east Ulster, replaced the landed class, Ulster unionism became more self-reliant. Up to 1900, however, unionism functioned as a formidable movement because of the effective cooperation between Irish landowners and northern business leaders. These emerging middle-class figures, many of whom had extensive industrial interests, were growing more anxious about the damage that Home Rule would inflict on the province's economic prospects. Indeed, there was considerable speculation that a number of Belfast's leading firms, including Harland and Wolff, would re-locate in Britain should Home Rule be enacted. While these economic concerns were undoubtedly genuine, it was the religious factor that proved most successful in mobilising Protestant opinion in the north. Thus, 'Home Rule means Rome rule' became the rallying cry of

Ulster unionism.

While the broader Unionist family tolerated this appeal to sectarian tribalism in times of crisis, it could cause acute embarrassment among Unionist supporters in Britain and the rest of Ireland. For Conservatives, the key issue was the threat that Home Rule posed to the Empire, a concern which was shared by southern Unionists. In truth, outside the family connections, Conservatives cared little for Ireland. While they identified strongly with Ulster resistance to Home Rule in 1886 and 1893, it was apparent that much of their defiance was reserved for periods when they were out of office. Although the fight against Home Rule strengthened the bonds between British Conservatives and Irish Unionists, each group was careful to protect its independence. Irish Unionists were never subject to the rigid discipline that Parnell imposed on the IPP and, during long periods of Conservative rule, Unionist MPs sometimes acted in a disunited and haphazard fashion. Any threat to the Union, however, led to a rapid closing of ranks. Still, most Unionist MPs showed little interest in British affairs. As the great majority of these MPs were Ulster Unionists, the term 'Ulster party' was often used to describe this distinctive Westminster grouping. While they were viewed as the Conservative party's natural allies and though they enjoyed some influence with the Conservative party, particularly with Lord Salisbury, these 'Ulster party' MPs were consistently wary of placing too much trust on their Tory allies. In fact, one historian has described the Ulster Unionist relationship to the British state as 'contractarian'. Unionists had colonised Ulster in the seventeenth century on England's behalf and, if the British state now reneged on its part of the 'contract' by imposing Home Rule and betraying Unionists to their enemies, then they would be absolved from any obligation to obey Westminster's laws. Thus, unionism, or loyalism, was based on an external relationship to the British state, rather than any real feeling of belonging to the British nation.

While this argument may have some merit, it does not take sufficient account of the growing sense of Britishness felt by many Unionists at the end of the nineteenth century. Indeed, unionism had also borrowed heavily from the ideology of late nineteenth-century British imperialism, which focused on the civilising impact of British rule and fitted neatly with ideas of Anglo-Saxon Protestant superiority. This allowed Unionists to undermine the nationalist argument that Home Rule enjoyed overwhelming support in Ireland and cast some doubt on the suitability of the Catholic Irish for self-government.

Unionist unity, then, was conditioned by an assessment of the seriousness of the nationalist threat. When this subsided following the defeat of the second Home Rule Bill, class divisions within unionism quickly surfaced. At the heart of this upheaval was the long-running dispute between landlord and tenant, and this problem was particularly acute in Ulster. Although the effect of denominational differences within Protestantism had been reduced by religious developments in the second half of the nineteenth century and by the unifying influence of the Orange Order, it was still strong enough to cause disruption in the north. This meant that the sometimes difficult relationship between Church of Ireland landowners and their Presbyterian tenants could be further strained by perceptions surrounding these denominational loyalties. Unlike Catholics, who often viewed their landlords as foreign oppressors, Presbyterian tenants had allied with the northern gentry in galvanising Unionist opposition to Home Rule. These Ulster tenants now expected to reap the benefits of their political support. At the same time, however, the landed class, typified by the attitude of Saunderson, was determined to defend landlord rights. A potentially disastrous situation in Ulster's rural constituencies was only averted by the land reforms introduced by the Conservative government at Westminster. Ulster's Presbyterian tenant farmers found a champion in Thomas Wallace Russell who had become Liberal Unionist MP for South Tyrone in 1886. Building on his core support among Presbyterian farmers in rural Ulster, Russell launched a popular campaign in the winter of 1894–95 aimed at pressurising the Conservative government to deliver land reform. Naturally, this drew him into conflict with Saunderson and the other landlord MPs who held out against reform. Much of what Russell advocated was included in the Conservatives' 1896 Land Bill, but, angered by what he regarded as the uncaring attitude shown by northern landlords to their Presbyterian tenants, he continued to press for radical changes. Yet Russell was distinguished by his ability as well as his radicalism. Both Arthur Balfour and Joseph Chamberlain held him in high regard, and he was regularly invited to Britain to speak on behalf of Conservative candidates engaged in by-elections. In 1895 he was appointed as a junior minister in the Local Government Board, but ministerial office failed to dilute his radicalism on the land question. When he began a new wave of land agitation in the late summer of 1900, he was dismissed from the government. Much to Saunderson's horror, Russell was now advocating compulsory land purchase, and this led to a serious rift between him and other Unionist MPs.

Although he was isolated by the leadership, Russell could not be ignored as his agitation for further land reform continued to attract tenant farmer support. By 1901 he had established his own organisation, with the intention of mounting an electoral campaign against Unionists. This move was successful, as Russellite candidates overturned Unionist majorities in the East Down and North Fermanagh by-elections in 1902–03. In both of these contests, victory was guaranteed by the action of Catholic tenant farmers who joined with their Presbyterian counterparts to defeat the Unionist candidates. Earlier, Saunderson, in spite of his impeccable Orange credentials, had found himself under serious pressure in holding off an independent opponent in his

North Armagh seat in the general election of 1900. There was widespread disaffection among North Armagh's tenant farmers, and the Unionist leader was accused of neglecting his constituents during his 15 years as their representative. Yet the class politics that Russell had championed could not survive. The shock of the 'devolution crisis' of 1904–05 once again raised the prospect of Home Rule, and Russell's electoral base was rapidly eroded as Unionists appealed for solidarity in the face of this perceived nationalist threat. It was the bourgeois element within Ulster unionism that led the fight back against Russellism. These middle-class leaders had been alarmed by Saunderson's failure to repel the Russellite challenge, and they were convinced that unionism desperately needed to find some way of channelling popular opinion. Their actions led to the appearance of a more localised form of unionism which sidelined Saunderson and his landowning colleagues. Indeed, Saunderson's position had been further undermined by a sustained attack from the populist Protestant leader Thomas Sloan, who won the South Belfast seat in a 1902 by-election and held it against the official Unionist challenger until 1910. Sloan, who enjoyed the support of loyalist ultras in Belfast, had savagely criticised Saunderson for being soft on Catholicism, and he led a breakaway faction to form the Independent Orange Order in 1903. One consequence of these political developments around the turn of the century was the formation of the Ulster Unionist Council (UUC) in 1905, a body that ensured much greater grass-roots participation within unionism and guarded against the threat of internal division.

The establishment of the UUC had shifted the focus within unionism towards a more representative and localised movement. Unionism ceased to be a predominantly parliamentary movement as the bourgeois element in Ulster seized the initiative. While the possibility of a rift between northern and southern unionism was now more likely, this was averted until the pressure of the next Home Rule crisis in 1913. Still, the logic of a more cohesive, popular movement in the north, which the new leaders deemed essential for Unionist electoral survival, was the development of a more self-reliant movement, less concerned with the particular problems facing Unionists in the south. Up to 1900, however, landlord influence, though in decline, ensured that unionism was, for the most part, united. Southern Unionists had enjoyed a disproportionate influence and this helped to ensure regional harmony, while the emphasis on parliamentary activity allowed Unionists to develop close links with their British Conservative allies. Russell's agrarian campaign in rural Ulster had highlighted damaging social divisions within the movement, but the emerging bourgeois leadership in the north eventually responded and managed to restore solidarity. In overcoming the Russellite threat and re-establishing class consensus within northern unionism, these new middle-class leaders had found a local solution to a local problem. Indeed, Saunderson and the old landed elite were increasingly irrelevant to the construction of a more dynamic populist movement, which encouraged greater grass-roots participation and was more suited to the changing demands of people politics. If Saunderson and his landed colleagues were now considered peripheral figures, so too were southern Unionists. It was among southern Unionists that the decline of Irish landlordism was most keenly felt. The gentry class had been the driving force within southern unionism, particularly outside Dublin, but the steady erosion of landlord power towards the end of the nineteenth century weakened the movement, both politically and financially. The problems facing southern Unionists reinforced the determination of Ulster's new middle-class leadership to take more responsibility for their own security.

There were, however, other problems undermining southern unionism. Southern Unionists were divided on the best strategy to maintain the Union. More enlightened elements favoured some kind of accommodation with moderate nationalists, but they faced a larger group of rejectionists who frowned on all attempts at reconciliation. The key figure among the moderates was Horace Plunkett, the MP for South Dublin. Plunkett was convinced that economic progress based on improvements in agriculture would overcome political division in Ireland. While he was firmly opposed to Home Rule, Plunkett advocated a progressive strategy aimed at reconciling the nationalist population to the Union. The key for Plunkett was wholesale improvements in agriculture which, he argued, would transform the Irish economy and lead to a reassessment of the Union. Before entering politics Plunkett had been a prime mover in the establishment and development of the Irish cooperative movement. Its aim was the modernisation of agricultural processing and marketing, through the creation of a large number of mini-enterprises which were funded by the pooling of local capital. Plunkett's vision was of a reconstructed rural economy and society which, ultimately, would radically alter attitudes to the national question. But Plunkett extended the principle of cooperation beyond the opening of new creameries. Following the general election of 1895, in which he retained his South Dublin seat, Plunkett called for representatives of both nationalism and unionism to meet for a discussion on the future economic development of Ireland. With a Conservative government in place at Westminster and Home Rule off the agenda, Plunkett assumed that the timing was right for his initiative. Although there was opposition from Unionist and nationalist leaders, a Recess Committee, so called because it met during the parliamentary recess of 1895–96, met to explore issues of common concern.

In 1896 the Recess Committee published a unanimous report, suggesting that consensus politics might replace the old divisions. The Recess Committee endorsed Plunkett's demand for the creation of a department of agriculture in Ireland and the provision of technical instruction. Certainly, the Conservative administration at Westminster was encouraged by the work of the Recess Committee. The new cross-party spirit of cooperation fitted neatly with the Conservative policy of 'constructive unionism' which ran from 1895 to 1905. This was the Conservative response to the Liberals' Irish strategy, and its aim was to achieve steady economic and political progress on a broad front in a way that would undermine the nationalist demand for Home Rule and reconcile a majority of Irishmen to the Union. Gerald Balfour, the Chief Secretary for Ireland from 1895 to 1900, had coined the phrase, "killing Home Rule with kindness", and he shared Plunkett's view that a commitment to economic improvements, particularly in agriculture, could rob nationalism of much of its appeal. Recent scholarship has cast doubt on the existence of such a coherent philosophy within constructive unionism, suggesting that much of the legislation introduced by Balfour and his successor, George Wyndham, should instead be seen as a series of pragmatic responses to particular problems around the turn of the century. Still, there had been a long history of British statesmen, notably Peel and Gladstone, pursuing constructive policies with the intention of ameliorating Irish conditions and, in so doing, limiting the economic appeal of nationalism. Indeed, most leading nationalists were convinced that Balfour's programme represented a direct threat to Home Rule. Dillon refused to sit on the Recess Committee, and he warned fellow nationalists to avoid being sidetracked from the legislative goal of Home Rule by the allure of consensus politics. Only the Liberal alliance could, he argued, deliver Home Rule, and he was highly suspicious of Conservative or Unionist requests for cooperation.

Dillon's caution meant that he was slow to recognise the significance of Balfour's 1898 Local Government Act, which allowed the Irish party to gain control over most county, urban and district councils, particularly in the three southern provinces. In the following year, Balfour introduced the necessary legislation to implement the recommendations contained in the Recess Committee's report. Suitably impressed by Plunkett's detailed knowledge of agriculture, Balfour created a new Department of Agriculture and Technical Instruction, and installed Plunkett as the body's first vice president. Earlier, Balfour's 1896 Land Bill had provided additional funds for land purchase and removed some of the obstacles discouraging tenants from buying their farms under previous legislation. Of course, the high point of the Conservative administration's land purchase policy was the 1903 Wyndham Act. It transformed Irish society by turning huge numbers of tenants into owner-occupiers, but, contrary to Conservative hopes, it failed to check nationalist impetus. Plunkett's vision of new consensus-style politics and cross-party cooperation, set against a background of growing economic prosperity based on the modernisation of Irish agriculture, had proved too optimistic.

For his part, Saunderson was dismayed by the Conservatives' betrayal of Irish landlordism. He viewed the land legislation as concessions to agrarian agitators who would never be satisfied, and he consistently used his influence with Salisbury to curb the reformist tendencies of the Conservative administration. Naturally, Saunderson had also been angered by Plunkett's unorthodox brand of unionism, and he shared Dillon's suspicions of the Recess Committee and consensus politics. Although a landlord himself, Plunkett's constant criticism of his fellow landlords enraged the Unionist leader. In fact, Plunkett's attitude and his reformist zeal also infuriated many of his constituents, and he lost his South Dublin seat at the 1900 general election due to the intervention of an independent Unionist candidate. Plunkett's political demise had demonstrated that southern unionism was not powerful enough to accommodate both reformist and mainstream factions. Still, in these formative years from 1885 to 1900, southern Unionists exerted a major influence on the new political movement. Social confidence and political know-how meant that the landed gentry were first to react to the Home Rule threat, while enthusiasm for the Unionist cause was evident among all sections of the Protestant community in Dublin. Consequently, unionism was essentially an Irish movement during these early years, and it was effective because of the easy relationship between Irish landlords and Ulster bourgeoisie. In time, however, these regional and class differences would become more pronounced, and it would become more difficult to hold this broad Unionist alliance together. The threat posed by Russell had undoubtedly added to this difficulty. In the end, it was Ulster's unique experience of industrialisation and, more particularly, northern Protestant control of this experience, which gave unionism a much more obvious Ulster focus in the early years of the twentieth century.

Conclusion

D EVELOPMENTS IN BRITISH POLITICS early in the twentieth century appeared to have rescued nationalism from the self-inflicted damage of the Parnellite split. After its long period of domination, the Conservative party had quarrelled with itself on the issue of tariff reform, bringing the Liberals back to power. Initially, with such a commanding majority, there was little incentive for the Liberal government to take any further risks on Irish Home Rule. However, this situation changed in 1910, when two further general elections produced hung parliaments. The Liberals continued in government, but they relied on the IPP for an overall majority. With the IPP holding the balance of power, the prospects for Home Rule appeared bright, and Dillon's faith in the Liberal alliance was vindicated. Moreover, the eruption of a constitutional crisis had led to the 1911 Parliament Act, which removed the Lords' veto and cleared the main obstacle to Home Rule. A third Home Rule Bill duly followed in 1912 and, with Westminster politics now poisoned by the controversy surrounding the constitutional crisis, the Conservative party gave its full backing to Unionist plans for opposition.

Still, constitutional nationalism appeared to be within touching distance of success, and all threats of Unionist resistance were dismissed as fanciful. At this point the Unionists found a champion who would channel popular Unionist opposition. Edward Carson had clearly learned from Parnell, and the style of militant constitutionalism that he deployed was reminiscent of Parnellism in its most effective early years. Yet though he was born in Dublin, Carson had no alternative but to sacrifice his Irish unionism and abandon his fellow southern Unionists, when the tough decisions had to be made in 1913. By this stage power within unionism clearly rested with the Ulster bourgeoisie, and this new leadership was less interested in the concerns of southern Unionists. Perhaps it was inevitable that the regional and class differences, which unionism had done well to control, would ultimately split the movement. Therefore, a partitionist approach to the Irish question, which had its origins in the formation of the UUC in 1905, became widely canvassed and, by 1921, such a compromise appeared to many, both in Ireland and Britain, as the only practical solution. Though expedient, partition created new problems for the traditional minorities in Ireland, the northern Catholics and the southern Protestants.

World War One damaged constitutional nationalism by delaying the implementation of Home Rule. At the same time, war encouraged violent nationalism. At Easter 1916, Fenians would seize the opportunity to strike a blow for Irish freedom while British attention was firmly focused on the western front. The insurrectionists looked forward to the establishment of an independent Irish state, but they also looked back by adding the 1916 rising to the list of previous rebellions. Hence, 1916 was intended to become part of the revolutionary nationalist tradition, with direct links to 1798, 1803, 1848 and 1867. Although the rising was a military disaster, the political objectives of the leaders were partly met. They provoked a British reaction which, in spite of wartime pressures, was viewed by Irishmen as an overreaction. Consequently, a rebellion that was characterised by a lack of popular support in what might have been considered favourable circumstances, received a retrospective endorsement from the people. This was quickly translated into political support for Sinn Fein, which swept aside the IPP in the post-war general election. Thus, another objective of the insurrectionists, namely the obliteration of the IPP, was achieved. When the British refused to acknowledge the reality of the new situation in Ireland, a guerrilla war with the aim of forcing a British withdrawal ensued. Nationalism had undergone a process of radicalisation, but this too would pass. By the summer of 1921 both the British government and Sinn Fein were seeking to break the cycle of violence. In the negotiations which followed the truce, the Irish accepted dominion status, thereby putting the new Irish Free State on a constitutional par with Canada. Looking back from 1921, it is easy to assume that the collapse of the Union was inevitable, but this can be misleading.

The Union was not a success and it eventually fell victim to the forces of revolutionary nationalism. Still, the fact that it lasted for 120 years suggests that it was not doomed from the outset. It had worked for Scotland and Wales, and both of these countries had a legacy of past conflict with England. Cultural nationalism had been particularly strong in Wales, but it did not develop into a political demand for Welsh independence. Yet, when cultural nationalism emerged in Ireland, it could not, despite the efforts of its early leaders, remain separate from political nationalism. Scotland had, of course, suffered terribly at the hands of the English in the eighteenth century. The unsuccessful attempt by 'Bonnie Prince Charlie's' Jacobite forces to seize the British Crown unleashed savage reprisals by the English government. In 1746 the remnants of the Jacobite army were slaughtered on Culloden Moor, and this was followed by the Highland clearances. The Scottish clan system was ruthlessly broken up, but this did not provoke a nationalist challenge to the 1707 Act of Union between England and Scotland. Instead, the Westminster government raised Highland regiments for the British army and this diverted the energies of the clansmen. More importantly, the government oversaw huge economic changes in Scotland which raised the general standard of living and helped Scots to become assimilated into the United Kingdom, while retaining their strong sense of national identity.

This did not happen in Ireland. Here, there were obvious geographical complications, but this alone does not explain the failure to absorb the Irish into the United Kingdom. One obvious problem was the absence of industrialisation outside north-east Ulster. Ireland did not, therefore, enjoy her share of the spectacular economic growth which much of Britain experienced in the nineteenth century. While most economic historians are agreed that the Union was not a serious factor inhibiting Ireland's economic development, the perception among nationalists was very different. True, rapid industrialisation had also been confined to specific areas in Scotland and Wales, but the Irish experience was more complicated. The fact that northern Protestants enjoyed a near-monopoly of the economic benefits accruing from industrialisation did not go unnoticed by nationalists. More crucially, the economic downturn in mid-nineteenth-century Ireland was in sharp contrast to developments in Britain, and the catastrophic impact of the famine further highlighted these differences.

In responding to all of these problems, the British offered too little, too late. The best example of this was Catholic emancipation. When it failed to appear as an addendum to the Act of Union, Catholics were presented with a clear grievance which, in time, they would seek to redress. Consequently, as far as the politically-conscious Catholic middle class was concerned, the Union operated with a clear Protestant bias. Indeed, the British government frequently found itself in a dilemma, caught between attempts to support a loyal Protestant minority and efforts to conciliate the less loyal Catholic majority. As the Catholic population was stereotyped as troublesome in this formative period, British policy consistently favoured the loyalists. In the end, it took a colossal effort to gain Catholic emancipation, which had become a symbol for Catholic grievances in general. It was the struggle for emancipation that created the Catholic political nation. In the process, Catholics ceased to be the passive people they had been at the time of the Union. Emancipation whetted Catholic appetites for further concessions, and new demands followed. Not surprisingly, Catholics believed that their suffering was due to their religion, and this provided a powerful impetus for the development of constitutional nationalism. Previously, nationalism had been the preserve of the politicised middle class, but the particular circumstances of the 1820s transformed it into a mass movement. This would be repeated in the last quarter of the nineteenth century, when the land issue mobilised the masses. Under O'Connell's leadership, Catholicism and nationalism became inseparable. This was a logical step, because O'Connell was quick to recognise that success in electoral politics required the active participation and support of the Catholic clergy.

Yet it is also important to stress the significance of Protestant nationalism, even though the numbers engaged were never large. O'Connell had a degree of Protestant support, while both the Young Irelanders in the 1840s and the early Home Rulers in the 1870s relied on Protestant leadership. A number of historians have suggested that the actions of this Protestant avant-garde within nationalism was an attempt by Protestants to stake a claim for leadership in a future Ireland which had achieved some measure of freedom from Britain. Davis fitted this bill, as did Parnell. Under Parnell's leadership nationalism, which had been in the doldrums since the early 1840s, recovered to become the dominant force in Irish politics. Indeed, the impact of the land agitation in 1879 marked a crucial turning point for constitutional nationalism. The Land League was the single most important movement in the development of nationalism.

Unlike the Catholic Association, the Land League was a movement initiated by the masses, who had united in opposition to an alien landlord class, to redress the major economic grievance of land tenure. After some hesitation, Parnell was awakened to the movement's potential, and he set out to control this new force and use it for his political ends. The land issue had mobilised the masses and, by linking the politics of Home Rule to the politics of land reform, Parnell won overwhelming popular support for a new style of constitutional nationalism. Both inside and outside Parliament, Parnell made this nationalism a confident, aggressive force, but the need to seek political allies at Westminster eventually smoothed nationalism's radical edge. Yet Parnell had succeeded in establishing a broad nationalist front, based on the fusion of agrarian and political forces. Although he was a conservative on social matters, the land agitation held out the prospect, at least for a brief period, of radical social change in Ireland, but this was not supported by the tenant farmers who wanted to own their holdings. When the government facilitated this, nationalism also shed its radical social edge.

Moreover, Parnellism was effective because it embraced constitutional Fenianism. Even in 1886, when the limitations of a Home Rule settlement were finally exposed, constitutional separatists could take comfort from the belief that the door to full independence had been opened. The readiness with which separatists engaged in constitutional politics was neither surprising nor new. Conversely, throughout the century, mainstream nationalists often engaged in militant rhetoric while paying homage to Ireland's revolutionary tradition. On the other hand, revolutionary nationalism could feed off constitutional nationalism, as the Young Irelanders had done with the Repeal movement. There was, therefore, some overlap between constitutional and revolutionary nationalism, but it was the constitutional strain that proved much more powerful, a fact which the ultimate success of revolutionary nationalism in 1916–21 has obscured. Indeed, it may not even be accurate to speak of a revolutionary tradition in nineteenth-century Ireland. Attempts by violent nationalists to secure Irish freedom were isolated and sporadic. Furthermore, the use of the term rebellion to describe the 1803 and 1848 incidents seems inappropriate given the small numbers involved and their negligible impact. While the famine gave some impetus to revolutionary nationalism, this was most keenly felt among the Irish diaspora in the United States. The subsequent emergence of the Fenian movement on both sides of the Atlantic involved more serious preparation for revolutionary activity, though recent research has cast some doubt on the revolutionary commitment of the Fenian membership in Ireland. Yet revolutionary nationalist movements such as Fenianism did raise the spectre of serious violence in Ireland or, even worse, Britain, if suitable concessions to Catholic nationalism were either rejected or delayed, and the most effective nationalist leaders were those constitutionalists who understood how to milk this threat. One British statesman who took revolutionary nationalism seriously was Gladstone. Initially, he sought to remove its causes through a programme of social and economic improvements, but eventually came to the conclusion that only Home Rule would pacify Ireland. Believing that all other possibilities had been exhausted, Gladstone was prepared to split his party on Ireland, though he remained confident that the Irish could be assimilated like the Scots in the previous century. The subsequent constitutional concessions made to Sinn Fein caused many members of the British establishment to rue the rejection of Gladstone's Home Rule Bills.

The tenant farming class had prospered under constitutional nationalism, as the land problem had been resolved to their satisfaction. Indeed, the need to respond to the agitation of the

United Irish League had been an important factor in the framing of the Wyndham Act. The Catholic middle class, particularly the business and commercial elements, had also benefited from the economic upturn in the last two decades of the nineteenth century, and they fully expected to play a prominent role in a Home Rule Ireland. These groups were not, to any real extent, interested in any possible cultural dimension of nationalism. Here, Ireland did not conform to the European pattern in which a cultural awakening preceded political nationalism. Instead, those who were drawn to cultural nationalism in Ireland rejected the process of modernisation welcomed by political nationalists. In fact, the pace of change towards the end of the century had caused upheaval and uncertainty within Irish society, a state of affairs that left one section of the people desperately searching for some kind of stability. Most of those who felt insecure as a result of these social, economic and cultural changes had not previously engaged with political nationalism, and this accounts for a new cadre of activists whose instinct was to stay aloof from conventional politics. Their dilemma was that Ireland did not have a rich cultural heritage to defend. This meant that much of their energy was spent on attacking English society and culture. In the end, cultural nationalists had to come off their pedestal, as they were increasingly drawn towards more radical forms of political nationalism.

Unionism was slow to respond to the challenge of Parnellism, and it was only when Home Rule appeared imminent that it organised its parliamentary forces. Once a decision was taken, however, unionism took advantage of the building blocks already in place. To function as an effective political movement unionism welded together the Protestant forces of the Irish Conservative party, the Church of Ireland and the Orange Order. Initially, a significant body of Protestants had opposed the Union, but, as the century progressed, defence of the Union became increasingly bound to the Protestant interest. Undoubtedly, the impact of O'Connellism and the advance of the Catholic political nation had forced a reassessment of Protestant political thinking. Of course, O'Connell also presented a new electoral challenge, and it was the Tory response to O'Connellism that forged the essential element in the birth of unionism. For most of the nineteenth century pro-Union candidates enjoyed a majority of Irish representation, but the emergence of a Home Rule party decisively shifted the balance of power. Previously, the restricted franchise enabled pro-Union candidates to win seats all over Ireland, but the general elections of 1885–86 suddenly raised the Ulster profile of the Irish Unionist movement. In spite of its bleak electoral prospects, southern Unionists continued to play a prominent, and perhaps dominant, role within unionism until 1900. The influence of the landed class combined with Saunderson's leadership ensured that unionism remained an Irish phenomenon during this period. The landed influence also facilitated the alliance with British Conservatism, though, on both sides, this was essentially determined by political opportunism rather than ideology. Naturally, the north's experience of industrialisation became a powerful feature of Ulster unionism, but the comfortable relationship between Irish landlordism and Ulster business during these early years largely obscured any regional variation within unionism. A more self-reliant Ulster unionism did not emerge until after the bourgeois takeover of the leadership in the early years of the twentieth century. Unionism cannot be dismissed as a purely negative movement. It was a complex coalition of different social groups and denominations held together by a common interest. In times of crisis the task of holding this coalition together was relatively straightforward, but class tensions quickly surfaced once the threat of Home Rule receded. To overcome this unionism developed a populist rhetoric which made any compromise with nationalism unlikely.

Index

Other books by the same author:

Ireland and British Politics (Colourpoint 1993)
Union to Partition, Ireland 1800–1921 (Colourpoint 1995)
Ireland 1905–25 Volume 1 (Colourpoint 1998)